FOLLOWING THE FÜHRER

A YOUNG GERMAN'S DIARY

FOLLOWING THE FÜHRER

A YOUNG GERMAN'S DIARY

by

Ingeborg Grant

CENTRAL PUBLISHING LIMITED
West Yorkshire

This is a true story. However, in order to protect persons mentioned
in this book, their names have been changed.

Paperback ISBN 1 903970 07 5

**Published
by**

Central Publishing Limited
Royd Street Offices
Milnsbridge
Huddersfield
West Yorkshire
HD3 4QY

www.centralpublishing.co.uk

INDEX

Foreword

When I came to England in 1951 barely two years had elapsed since my release from Buchenwald, one of a number of Schweigelager – Silent Concentration Camps - the Russians had maintained in the DDR since 1945.

The memory of the suffering of these years was still very fresh in my mind and I wanted the world to know what had happened on Stalin's order, but I never wrote my story.

In the years that followed I learnt more and more about the horrors and unthinkable crimes that had been perpetrated by the system which I had supported, crimes, no doubt, ordered by the man I had idolized.

My feelings about my own fate changed. The outrage once felt at the indiscriminate imprisonments and the destruction of thousands of mostly innocent people, has given way to the realisation that far greater crimes had been committed in the name of the German people.

When, at a later stage, the diary which I had kept from 1937 to 1940 came to light I lacked the courage to open it and it was not until I reached retiring age and found myself with leisure time at my hands that I re-read my early musings. I read sometimes with surprise and not always with pride what the person I once was had done and thought.

The idealism which guided my young years, I can neither deny nor alter even if views and opinions have changed as my life took its course.

As I look back over the first almost 30 years of my life I can see them as a tiny slice of history and so I decided to write my story, built around my diary entries, for anyone who may be interested to read.

1997
England

Following The Führer
A Young German's Diary

THE FAMILY

21ˢᵗ January, 1933

My name is Ingeborg and today is my 10ᵗʰ birthday. From now on I will keep a diary but first I will say a little about myself and my family.

We live in a flat, my Grandad, my Uncle Henry (I call him Henry because he is only a student), my Mum and Dad and my brother Jurgen. Our flat is quite large, our landlord lives downstairs and I was born in the smaller flat, upstairs.

My brother is younger than me, he is all right but we often fight each other.

My Dad is very good to us, but he does not play with us because he is too old, nearly 50. He works in a bank in Berlin but when he was young he wanted to be a teacher only he could not. His dad had died very young and his mum could not afford to send him to college. He and his brother, my Uncle Paul, had to earn money as soon as possible.

My Mum looks after us all and I think it must be hard for her because when she was a young girl she did not have to work. She had nice friends and went to balls and had a good time.

My Mum's dad, my Grandad, did not have to work either. He had a lot of money and two houses in Berlin. He collected butterflies and caterpillars. In our store-rooms upstairs there are lots of boxes with dead butterflies and caterpillars all with Latin names attached and my Mum says my Grandad wrote books about them and gave them names if nobody had done so before.

My Mum's grandad was a millionaire and had a villa in Lankwitz. Lankwitz is now a part of Berlin but when my Mum was a little girl and her grandad sent his coach and horses, they drove across fields to get to the villa.

My Grandad and his father lost all their money in 1914 when the Great War started, but I don't know whether they lost it because of the war.

My uncles Walter and Werner became soldiers during that war. My Mum says that all the young men volunteered to join the Army and they marched through Berlin and sang and the girls threw flowers and waved and everybody thought the war would soon be over. My Dad, though, did not join up because his heart was not good and he was not wanted. I don't think he was very happy.

I heard someone say that my Mum was engaged to a rich man but when her family was suddenly poor he did not want to marry her. It must have been very sad for my Mum.

It was then that my grand-parents moved to Mahlow and into the flat.

Mahlow is a suburb of Berlin but is not part of it. Sometimes we take the steam train to go shopping in Berlin. It takes only half an hour to the Potsdamer Platz.

On Sundays we often go for a walk across the fields and woods to our village and we pass the pond where we can skate in the winter.

In 1914 my Grandad had to start earning money and he found a job in an Apothecary, dispensing medicines. When one of us is not well we never call a doctor because my Grandad knows all about medicines and brings what we need.

My Mum too had to go out to work. She found a job in an office, something to do with statistics.

When my Mum and Dad got married they rented the small flat upstairs, where I was born. At that time there was a bad inflation, it was because Germany lost the war and had to pay a lot of money to the other countries. The Kaiser had abdicated and nobody knew what to do. A loaf of bread was 1000 marks and the next day it could cost twice as much and the money people earned was worth nothing.

A couple of years ago my Grandmother died. I loved her very much. I remember when we went on our summer holidays and my Grandma came to the station to see us off. I cried so much that people in the train thought something dreadful had happened.

When I was very small my parents wanted me to do exercises every day. It was because they wanted me to be strong and not suffer from a bad heart like my Dad. So I went to my Grandma every afternoon and we played wheelbarrow – she was holding my legs and I walked on my hands round and round the dining table. For every round I got one chocolate drop.

Now we are all living in Grandad's flat so that my Mum can look after us all.

CHILDHOOD

28th January, 1933

There will be another election on Sunday. It is fun having elections. Jurgen and I collect all the leaflets from the many parties. We think Hindenburg is the best because he was a great general in the war, but we heard my parents say that this time they will vote for Hitler and his National Socialist German Party. They think he has new ideas and all the other parties have failed.

31st January, 1933

Hitler's party has had the most of the votes and Hitler is now Chancellor. They say there has been much celebrating in Berlin with a torch-light march to the Chancery. We had some celebrations here but I missed them because Jurgen and I had to go to bed.

February, 1933

When my aunt came to lunch last Sunday – she comes every Sunday – she was wearing a badge and said she is a member of Hitler's party and that Hitler is very good, he will find jobs for everybody. I know my Dad is always worried about his job. I think Hitler must be a good man.

March, 1933

I shall be going to a new school in Berlin after Easter because I cannot learn much more in our village school. We should have had to pass an entry examination but the new Government has cancelled that – jolly good!

My cousin Traute will go to the same school. She is only two months younger than myself and we are almost like sisters. She has a brother Harry but he is only 7. They live only a few streets away from us.

April, 1933

My new school is very good. I have to travel by train every day but only to the next stop. The school is in a large building, half of it is occupied by the boys' grammar school. During the breaks we go out into the yard. We use one side of it, the boys the other. There is no dividing fence but nobody every steps over to the other side.

We learn French now, English will follow two years later.

May, 1933

We all lined the streets yesterday because Hitler was passing through. We waved as his car went by.

Today my great-aunt arrived to visit us. She lives in a village near Guben. She was very angry with my Mum. She said she would have given anything to see Hitler.

Thuringia, July, 1933

This is the long summer holiday and we are in Thuringia. We have been here many times before. Mum and Dad like it, the woods are lovely.

We stay in a house where we have rented a large room. We have breakfast in the garden. In the morning we often go and sit by a stream where Jurgen and I can play in the water. I love best picking blueberries and hearing the bells when the cows are gathered in the village and taken out onto the fields.

We shall be here for four weeks – not many children go away for such a long holiday.

October, 1933

We have a new friend. His name is Rudi. He is staying with his aunt and uncle in the flat upstairs. He is eleven years old and goes to the same school as I do – the boy's school, of course. He comes from a village 6 kilometres away and has to cycle to school, so during the winter he is allowed to stay with his aunt.

He is very good-looking and nice.

Mid-December, 1933

We spent the whole afternoon helping Mum baking Pfefferkuchen for Christmas. The dough was prepared some time ago- to be right it has to be in a warm place – on top of our stove. Our job is cutting out stars, angels, Father Christmases and so on – I always think this is the beginning of Christmas. Mum puts tray after tray into the oven. She is very clever because she has to heat the oven with coal and I don't know how she gets just the right heat. We bake such a lot of Pfefferkuchen because we are a large family and they all come to us on Christmas Day – I am looking forward to it.

17ᵗʰ December, 1933

Dad took us to our coal merchant today, because we buy our Christmas tree there. It has to be a big one, very high and it takes a long time to find a good tree. We took it home on our toboggan.

18ᵗʰ December, 1933

Our great-aunt Anna has arrived, she always comes to us for Christmas. We like her, she is jolly and has time to play card games with us. Rudi will be allowed to join us.

Christmas Even, Morning

At last it is Christmas, Mum closed the door to the lounge last night and Jurgen and I shall not be allowed into it until the evening. In the afternoon we shall be going to the cemetery to take flowers and branches from our tree to Grandma's grave. After that we shall go to our village church for the Christmas service. We never go to church on any other day. I love singing the Christmas hymns.

Christmas Eve

When we came home I was allowed to put on my new

dress – a lovely pink one, Mum made it. And then the door opened! The room looks quite different now, so full of Christmas - 24 candles were lit on the tree and all around the room there were tables with presents: for Jurgen and me and Mum and Dad, Grandad, Aunt Anna and my uncle Henry.

Christmas Day 1933

In the afternoon all my other aunts and uncles came for coffee and supper. There were 16 persons and even our large dining table is not big enough and we, the children, had to eat at a small table in the other room. I don't like that at all, I like listening to the grown-ups.

The other thing that spoils Christmas a bit is that after coffee, when we had our presents from the aunts and uncles, we have to stand up and say the special Christmas poem which Mum taught us. I was so worried that I forget my lines. But I do like having so many visitors though it must be hard work for Mum.

January, 1934

We are in a new year, the Christmas tree will have to go now. I know it cannot stay forever but it is so sad. My parents move it when I am in bed and now there will be a long, long year before I can think of Christmas again.

21st January, 1934

It is my birthday and I am allowed to ask my new school friends to a party. One of my friends is Eileen, her parents have a very nice house in Mahlow.

Easter, 1934

I have finished my first year at the new school and my end of term report is not too bad.

We now have a garden, it is only a few minutes' walk from our flat. I think my parents took it on a few years lease. There are lots of fruit trees and a strawberry plot. We also have a little wooden house with two rooms where Mum can prepare supper for us.

Easter Sunday 1934

We had a lot of visitors today and took photographs in the garden. Mum has a camera; it is very complicated. She has to put glass plates into it – they are very heavy.

1st May 1934

This is going to be a day of celebrations because when Hitler called his party Nationalist Social Workers' Party, he meant that everybody, even housewives, are workers, so it is a day for all of us.

In Berlin all the offices are closed, but the workers were asked to assemble and march to the Templehof field where Hitler was to speak to them. Dad had to go too. I cannot really picture my Dad marching and singing. But when he came home he was quite happy and said it was all very impressive.

Friday, 18th May, 1934

They brought my Dad home last night – he went straight to bed – Mum said he was very ill. Then my uncle went off on his motorbike to find a doctor – he was away for a long time. I saw my Dad once through the open bedroom door, he did not move. Mum would not let us sleep in our beds, we slept in the lounge.

Mum came to wake us up this morning. She was very upset and said that our Dad was no longer with us and that we would have to be very brave but Dad would never have been well again.

23rd May, 1934

Today we were sent away to my aunt's place. I knew it was our Dad's funeral. When we came home there were lots of people with Mum. I noticed my uncle wore a black SS uniform. I wondered whether he borrowed it, he never said he joined the SS.

Monday, 28ᵗʰ May, 1934

I went back to school today. It was very strange, the other girls didn't know whether to speak to me or not.

I shall have to do well at school now. I am sure Mum will not have much money and only children with good reports have their school fees reduced.

Summer Holidays 1934

Rudi is staying with his aunt and uncle during the holidays and we play together every day. He comes to the garden with us.

October, 1934

Mum has joined the 'Red Cross'. They are very good organising plays and dances and every Christmas they put on a very popular show. Mum says she wants me to take part in the shows so that I overcome my fear of speaking in front of others - I have always been a bit shy. When I first went to school, Mum had to sit at the back of the classroom for the first few weeks so that I wouldn't run home.

But I think Mum has another reason – everybody is expected to belong to an organisation. The one for women is called the Frauenschaft, but Mum does not like political activities and hopes the Red Cross will save her.

I want to join the Hitler Youth but Mum has said 'no.'

Christmas Eve, 1934

I dreaded this Christmas, the first without Dad. I think we all dreaded it but all the preparations went ahead as always.

Tonight Mum dressed up as Father Christmas, I knew it was Mum but I pretended not to, it was all so awkward and sad.

Jurgen and I had a film projector and a film to go with it. We looked at it later in the evening. It was really quite funny because people walk in such an odd way. Mum said we must not talk much about the film, she got it from a distant relative of ours who is a Freemason. The Freemasons are a secret Society with many Jews and we are not supposed to have anything to do with them. But there are no other films about.

21st January, 1935

I had a bicycle for my birthday. A real proper bike! I am sure Mum had to pay about 30 marks for it and that is a lot of money. But in the summer Mum may allow me to cycle to school. It isn't all that far, 10 minutes or so down the road and through a small wood and another few streets. It would save the cost of a season ticket for the train.

February, 1935

I do miss my Dad so much. I often cry in bed but only if Mum cannot hear it. I would like to have a Dad and then I thought I would think of the Führer as my Dad. Nobody is to know about that but I would always be true to him.

March, 1935

I had another go at Mum. I want to join the Hitler Youth. For the 10-14 year old it is called the 'Bund Deutscher Mädchen' – BDM. All the girls in my class have joined, even Traute has and she is going camping with them soon. Mum has not promised yet, but I think she will give in. She will have a word with my aunt!

20th April, 1935

Mum has given in – hurray!

It is the Führer's birthday today and I am officially joining the BDM. Our uniform is a dark blue skirt and a white blouse – Mum made them for me. We will have to buy the brown jacket. We can also wear a cardigan – black with a green and red border. I hope I will get it as a

Christmas present. When I become a proper member in November I shall also be allowed to wear the black scarf held around the neck by a leather knot.

May, 1935
Jurgen now goes to the same school in Berlin.

We have started English lessons; I don't like our teacher and I don't like the sound of English but at least the grammar seems much simpler than ours.

July, 1935
My uncle Henry is very clever, he is only a student but he owns a motorbike and a boat on the Mellensee. There is a very small bathing place and the owner has allowed Henry to build a tiny hut amongst the reeds so that he can stay there on weekends.

Mum, Jurgen and I are going to his place for a few days and Henry is taking me on his motorbike – Jurgen is very envious! Mum will teach me to swim.

July, 1935
Rudi is staying with his aunt and uncle again. We are playing together in the garden all day and we have invented some wonderful games.

9th November, 1935
We had a special meeting today and now I am a proper 'Jungmädel'.

When we have our weekly meetings 'Heimabende' we learn a lot of things we are never taught at school. We hear about the Führer's life, how he joined the German army in 1914, even though he was an Austrian and how upset he was when Germany lost the war and the Kaiser had to abdicate. How he promised that he would do something to reverse all the punishment that was laid down in the Versaille Treaty. He wanted the German people to be proud again and respected in the world. And now we are proud to be the Führer's youth!

We also hear of the many German territories that we had to give to other countries and how the German people there want to return to Germany.

Sometimes we learn songs, some are marching songs which we shall sing on the special days like the 1st May and on the Führer's birthday when there are processions through the town. Others are folk songs which have survived for many generations; we are told to be proud of the ancient customs.

November, 1935
Mum must have had a word with the lady in charge of the Red Cross. I am in the Christmas show, one of four angels in long white dresses. We each carry a candle and after we have recited our poem we turn and light a candle on a large advent wreath.

Early December, 1935
Mum asked what I wanted for Christmas, I said 'the Führer's 'Mein Kampf'. Her reply was 'that is not a present for a young girl.' I said, 'I want nothing else.'

Saturday, 19th December, 1935
We had our Christmas show today. Our local pub has a large hall with a stage, the hall was full. I got through my lines without getting stuck but I had a terrible cold and almost lost my voice. They gave me lots of hot lemon drinks beforehand. But I had to clutch a large handkerchief as I went onto the stage – not very angelic! - and nearly got into trouble when I had to light the candle. I think a few laughs came from the audience.

Christmas Day, 1935
Christmas Eve was not quite as bad as last year, I think

Mum kept busy so that she did not have to remember. All the family came. My Grandad had a radio from his children. It is called a 'People's Receiver.' It is quite a small box with a loudspeaker built-in. We don't need earphones; one just plugs it into the electricity. How good that we now have electricity. Up to a few years ago we only had gas and I remember my Dad lighting the lamps with a match. It is so much easier and less dangerous now.

1st January, 1936

I think this year will be a very exciting one because the Olympic Games are to be held in Berlin. A new stadium is being built and also a whole new village for the competitors. Many foreigners will visit us.

February, 1936

We have a new English teacher. He is young, small and ugly and we all love him. We have a lot of fun when he tells us about his student days and his time in England. But when he decides that we had enough fun we get down to work and nobody would dream of interrupting.

May, 1936

We had very exciting news. The Olympic Games will be opened with a special performance called 'Festival of Youth' on the evening of the first day. Many of the schools in Berlin will take part and our class has been chosen. I am not quite sure what we are to perform but we have already been told what dresses we need, very pretty ones with longish, flared skirts and we must start rehearsing straight away.

June, 1936

We have invented a new game in our garden. We are racing drivers on our bikes. Jurgen is Rosemeyer, Rudi is Carraciola and I am v. Brauchitsch. We race from the garden gate, down the middle path, around a raised bend, back along the fence and the garden hut. I am afraid during the last stage we often crash into the flower beds. Grandad loves putting little wooden fences around the beds and, of course, we break them. There is always trouble! Also Jurgen does not like me to win and he has invented tests I have to take including speed tests on the road. I never quarrel with Rudi.

July, 1936
Mum, Grandad, Jurgen and I are going away for a week's holiday in the Sächsische Schweiz, it is not far from Dresden.

Sächsische Schweiz, July, 1936
It is lovely here. We are staying at a bed and breakfast place. There is a family staying in the house next door. They have a son who must be about 15. He is already a leader in the Hitler Youth. He is very nice and I talk to him as often as I can, but I don't think he cares much about me.

21ˢᵗ July, 1936
This week we are rehearsing for the Olympics every day. We go by train to the stadium in the morning and last night it was dark when I came home. Mum waits for me at the station. Of course, for a lot of the time we are just waiting for our turn. We went to the swimming stadium and watched some of the competitors practising their dives from the highest board. It is all so interesting!

22ⁿᵈ July, 1936
Today Hermann Goering came to inspect the stadium. Word went around and we all ran to see and cheer him.

23ʳᵈ July, 1936
We saw the runner who will carry the Olympic flame into the stadium – even he has to rehearse.

It is all so wonderful, so exciting to be part of this great event.

The stadium has lots and lots of underground rooms and long passages – made to get lost in!

Our show is really taking shape; it is so cleverly thought out. One would have to see it looking down from a place in the stadium.

I may be very lucky. I am only a substitute and shall not be required at the dress rehearsal, but I have tickets for Mum and Jurgen and shall see the show with them.

28th July, 1936

Mum and Jurgen were so thrilled – I loved it too. The Festival is depicting the stages of human life. It opens with the young school children running in and forming the Olympic rings on the green grass. The representatives from different countries play and sing their traditional songs. Our dance follows, it is so effective: hundreds of girls in cream-coloured dresses with rust-brown ribbons moving in unison. Palucca, the famous solo dancer performed in our midst. After that hundreds of flags are carried into and around the stadium to the sound of the triumphal march from 'Aida'. The next picture introduces a serious note - a sword dance is followed by the mourning for the dead and for the finale a very large orchestra plays some wonderful music, the choir and soloists join in – the singers are all famous soloists from the opera house. Whilst the music is playing a dome of light appears high above the stadium. I believe it is formed by anti-aircraft searchlights stationed at some distance.

We went home so happy, elated. What a wonderful time we live in!

Saturday, 1st August, 1936

The Führer opened the Olympic Games, he was greeted with an enormous ovation.

I was not required for the opening of our show but had to go along all the same – someone might have dropped out at the last moment – The Führer was there!

3rd August, 1936

It is wonderful that we have a radio. I spend most of the time in Grandad's room listening.

There will be two repeats of our show and I have already been told that I shall be 'on'. It looks as if some of the girls are losing interest.

6th August, 1936

We had our first repeat performance. As we were leaving the stadium we came quite close to the group of Italian singers – they are terribly handsome. Annerose – she is a very pretty girl – took all her courage and, egged on by us, stepped forward and said in French (we don't know any Italian) 'votre chancon était très bien!' They smiled – we felt really heroic.

9th August, 1936

We are winning so many medals, it is so good. Our athletes are inspired when the Führer is present!

There is a remarkable American athlete, Jesse Owen. He is a black man, everybody talks about him. He has won three gold medals.

16th August, 1936

The Games are over – I sat glued to the radio, couldn't tear myself away. I felt such a sense of loss – but it has been terrific!

End August, 1936

Back at school. Our teacher has made me Head Girl for our class. I cannot understand it; this job is usually given to the top girl and I am far from that. The problem is that we are quite naughty at times and now I shall have to stand up and speak for the others. He should have given the task to Val or Eileen, they are clever, they sit in the front row and whisper and giggle, yet know all the answers.

September, 1936

I have just found out that the wonderful music played as the finale to our Olympic show was Beethoven's 9th Symphony, the last movement.

My uncle has a gramophone with a large horn. It needs winding up and he sometimes plays records of Richard Tauber but he has no symphonies.

27th December, 1936

Christmas has been and gone. The whole family came as usual.

Jurgen and I had skis for Christmas. It was Jurgen who asked for them, so I thought I didn't want to be left out. They must have been very expensive for Mum; one needs so many things to go with them. I doubt whether I shall be very good at this sport. I hate speed and heights.

PRE-WAR YEARS

(Translated from the diary kept at the time)

30th January, 1937

I will make this the first entry in my new diary. I have chosen the day purposely.

The Führer has just finished his address to the German nation. Today, the four years are up. Four years he asked for to fulfil his promises. What great things he achieved! The communists have disappeared from Germany. The Saarland has returned. There is no unemployment. Our young men will do their National Service once more. Our soldiers returned to the Rhineland and, last but not least, the Führer has given back to us our self-respect. Today the Führer has, on behalf of our German people, withdrawn the signature with which we once accepted the sole responsibility for all the ills of the Great World War.

How proud we are to have such a Führer. How foolish of people not to trust him. There is nothing the Führer cannot do and he will never cause another war, as so many fear – unless it is unavoidable.

31st January, 1937

Last night I had to attend a public meeting to commemorate the day. The Führer's speech was repeated this morning on the radio – nobody can carry along an audience as he does.

Mum and Jurgen went off to Rangsdorf. Jurgen wanted to go skiing. I could not make up my mind and when I did they had gone.

4th February, 1937

We had our English essays returned. I had bad marks for translation but top marks for grammar.

7th February, 1937

Eileen and I went to the theatre in Berlin to see 'Götz von Berlichen' with Heinrich George. The play was good, the theatre awful.

15th February, 1937

I have been asked to attend a training course for future BDM leaders but Mum does not want me to go.

18th February, 1937

Mum will not let me go on the course and she won't let me take over a Schaft[1] either. She wants me at home, which I can understand. But I want it so much. Mum thinks I want it to show off but that is not the reason. I know it will require sacrifices and I shall not find it easy. But I want to do the Führer's work, want to help bringing up young people true to his ideas. Do I have to be denied what others are able to do, just for my mother's sake, because my father died so early?

21st February, 1937

It is all over, I am not attending the course, I shall not take on a Schaft. Mum says it would not be good for me. She maintains that I am often so insolent to her and others. I know that, but it only happens when they belittle the Führer. So I shall not help in his work. Mum says 'perhaps later' but I know that will not happen – it was a dream. I shall have to stay at home when the others go off. But I must not let Mum see how much it hurts me.

23rd February, 1937

Val says she will come and use all her powers to persuade Mum, but I wonder. Somehow I don't care anymore.

---

[1] Group of about 20 ten year olds, the lowest unit in the BDM.

28th February, 1937

It is Sunday and the radio is bringing the Request Concert. It goes non-stop from 5.00 p.m. to 10.00 p.m. Lots of people send in requests and DM26.000 have been donated for the Winter Aid fund. Many famous singers, Franz Völker, Fassbaender, Erna Berger, give their services free.

20th March, 1937

Today our new recruits have to register for the Hitler Youth. Val and I were on duty. We went to our meeting room, tidied up and decorated it to look smart and then took up our position – six candidates arrived – it was fun.

21st March, 1937

Today was Rudi's confirmation. We cycled across but Jurgen had a puncture and we had to stop twice to pump up the tyre. We reached Selchow very late, they were already eating lunch. Rudi looked very handsome. We had to depart at 6.00 p.m. to cycle the long way home.

12th April, 1937

Our Easter holidays are over. I went to the opera twice. Once with Mum to the Deutsche Opera to hear the 'Flying Dutchman'. It was my first visit to the opera; it was wonderful.

I also went to the Schiller Theatre to hear 'La Boheme'. It was only a school performance and not very exciting.

This will be a very busy week. Today we are singing for an hour in a public park so that people can see what we, in the BDM, are up to. Tomorrow is sport's night. Held in the hall at our local pub. Wednesday is rehearsal for the 20th – the Führer's birthday – and the 1st May celebrations.

16th April, 1937

This is the 'Week of the Young Germans' and we all have to contribute something to publicise the Youth movement. Eileen and Val's group performed an impromptu play framed by songs and folk dancing.

We shall be going to Berlin on the 20th – I am so excited!

20th April, 1937

The whole family went to Berlin to see Hitler's birthday parade. We secured a good place and saw at least some of the troops and we saw the Führer twice – we could hear the roar of the excitement coming nearer and nearer, getting louder all the time. Then the cars came into view. The Führer sat in the front car. Goering, Raeder, Blomberg followed. We had just started walking home across the park when the roar of the 'Heil' 'Heil' rose again.

We rushed back, tried to balance on the small railings and caught a sight of the Führer – he stood in the front of his car.

I had to go to the local celebrations in the evening. Because of the parade a lot of soldiers were accommodated in private houses around here, many of them came to the meeting.

1st May, 1937

What a wonderful day! I got my little group after all! I went to a meeting at 9.00 a.m. to hear the relay from the stadium. Before the meeting Hiddy asked me if I would like to take on a Schaft. She went immediately to my mother. I had expected to remain amongst my friends in Mahlow, but I will take over the one in Glasow and the girls will be of mixed ages. Never mind – the first gathering will be next Wednesday.

7th May, 1937

We heard the news that our airship 'Hindenburg' exploded just before landing in North America. They say it was not sabotage.

The day of the first meeting! It was pouring with rain, the sky was almost black and thunder and lightning were raging. I was alone in the house with my grandfather and not at all at ease. What should I do with the girls? It was supposed to be a sports meeting in the grounds of the school. At half-past four I left to cycle 10 minutes down the road. Once I was on my bike I felt so happy and free, I sang out loud racing along. But at the school I found the doors locked and nobody there. Eventually a teacher appeared, let me in but none of the girls arrived. I waited for 20 minutes and then made my way home – what a start!

27th May, 1937

I have already conducted three meetings with my girls. We are training for the National Youth Sports Competition.

It is so hot, we have been sent home early from school almost every day this week.

29th May, 1937

Sports day today. I came out almost top of the local league – only because I can throw a ball better than most.

31st May, 1937

Last night the Spanish Bolsheviks bombarded our 'Deutschland' warship, 23 died. What an outrage! German ships bombarded a Spanish harbour in retaliation.

4th June, 1937

It is now known that the aircraft which bombarded our 'Deutschland' was under orders from the Soviet Union. Everybody fears a war now – it won't happen!

We had a school outing to the exhibition 'Give me Four Years' – it was terribly good!

10th June, 1937

It is still so hot, we leave school early almost every day. I pick strawberries in the garden.

14th June, 1937

A lorry took us to Jüterbock, it was great fun. We sang all the way. We took part in the sports competition for the whole area – we won the relay – we are all overjoyed. The folk dancing we performed was not too good.

9th August, 1937

I have fallen behind with my entries. The summer holidays have been and gone, much has happened.

From 26th July to 4th August I attended a training course in the Youth Hostel in Liessen. It was wonderful. Val was there too; Irmela conducted the course, she is super. We got up at 6.30 every morning and out for a jog. Breakfast at 8.00 a.m. was followed by a morning of singing and lectures. After lunch at midday we were free until 2.30 when we gathered for a reading from the book 'And God is silent'. In the afternoon we had instructions in various crafts and more sport. After supper there were discussions, talks and singing. At the end of the day we met around the flagpole and with a short ceremony the flag was lowered.

At 9.30 when we were in bed and the lights off Irmela came around to say 'Good Night' and our three leaders completed the day with an evening song. It was always a moment for reflection except one night when a broom was knocked over with a loud crash and the three got the giggles and could not continue.

On Sunday afternoon we put on entertainment for the villagers. We performed the fairytale 'Der Schweinehirt' with Irmela in the title-role, she was so good!

On Monday and Tuesday we concentrated on getting our sports medal including a 25 km march. It was not as bad as we had feared.

These were wonderful days and we all felt very sad when it came to saying 'good-bye'. We learned so much that we shall need to work with our young girls. We realised what a responsibility has been placed on our shoulders.

23rd August, 1937

We went to the stadium to see the '700 Year Berlin' celebrations. There were scenes of all the important epochs of the 700-year history. The greatest applause went to the soldiers of Fredric the Great. They marched so smartly through the stadium. Very impressive was the 30-year war depicted by four horse-men: death, hunger, war and pest.

30th August, 1937

On Saturday we finally held the entry tests for our new girls. – last Saturday was rained off. They all passed the test – it was fun working with the youngsters.

8th September, 1937

We had a school outing to Potsdam and the palace 'Sansuci'. We – Val, Eileen, Traute and I – had planned to 'get lost'. It was difficult to find the right moment, but when the class turned right around the palace, we took a left turn and made straight for the exit. We stopped at a café and rejoiced in our freedom and then made our way to Val's grandmother, where, after telling a few fibs, we were treated to coffee and cakes. At the appointed hour we turned up at the station to meeting the rest of the class. A good telling-off followed! (Our absence must have been a worry to the teacher.)

9th September, 1937

Received another telling-off at school and were ordered to write an essay 'How to behave during a school outing'!

18th October, 1937

Mussolini has been in Berlin! We stood for two hours and at the last moment I was lucky, someone pushed from behind, got me onto a little elevation in the road and I had a free view ahead of me. I saw both Mussolini and the Führer perfectly, they both stood erect in their cars.

The following day Jurgen and Rudi went to Berlin to see the parade. They did not bother to tell me when they were leaving and had left when I woke up in the morning. This spoilt the whole day for me.

On Saturday my uncle Henry got married. Traute and I were bridesmaids. Mum made my dress, pale blue tulle; Traute's is a light-green organza. Two tiny toddlers carried the bride's veil and sat on the altar steps during the ceremony. They looked sweet! The reception was held at our local pub that has a big hall and a large garden. We had a sit-down dinner and dancing until the early hours. The parson came to the dinner and stayed for the dancing. He is quite a jolly man and a flirt too.

13th November, 1937

Eileen has been promoted. There has been a lot of gossiping at school – most of it is envy.

Two weeks ago I moved into my own room – the one Henry vacated. Mum was very secretive about it for a few days and then, on Sunday morning, I was solemnly taken into it. Mum performed miracles! White furniture, lovely, frilly curtains and a new couch. I am writing this in the seclusion of my own room – and by torchlight under the bed clothes! The light shining under the door would tell Mum that I am still awake.

5th February, 1938

On Christmas Eve Traute was taken ill with mumps. That spoilt our usual family gathering on Christmas Day.

I went down with mumps a few days later, Eileen and Val followed. We did not mind missing school but we were all to attend a conference in Luckenwalde on the 21st January – my birthday. We were desperate not to miss it because the new, very dashing leader of the boys Hitler Youth was to travel with us!

In January a new branch of the BDM was created 'Faith

and Beauty' (Glaube und Schoenheit.) It is for the 18 to 21 year old. As belonging to the Hitler Youth is now compulsory, it was difficult to keep the older girls interested. Now the emphasis will be on dance and culture and they will no longer have to wear the blue skirts, white blouses and brown jackets.

Yesterday, the 4th February, will go down in history as one of the most important dates in the National Socialist movement. Von Bomberg and Fritsch have resigned from their positions in the army. Goering is now Fieldmarshall. The Ambassadors to Vienna, Rome, Tokyo have been re-called. The Reichstag is to assemble on the 20th. Of course, many people think war is in the air, but I cannot believe that.

We don't know yet whether something really great is in the making, perhaps only our children will be able to judge and either condemn or praise. May the Almighty guide the Führer!

Sunday, 6th February, 1938

When we were sitting around the supper table with our Sunday guests the awkward subject of politics came up again, as so often. My uncle is so good and convincing in any argument. But this time I took the liberty of expressing my views. I was told to leave the room with the words 'this is not a subject for you!' I walked out fuming with rage. How I hate the words 'you don't understand that'. Unfortunately I had to struggle to keep back the tears.

9th February, 1938

At the meeting with my girls, some of the very young ones, who are due to join at Easter, attended – they are so sweet and keen. I wish I could lead a group of these 10-year olds!

We are planning our farewell party at school. After Easter I shall change to a school in Mariendorf for another three years to get my 'A' levels (*Abitur*).

I have chosen the branch that concentrates on domestic sciences with only one language.

14th February, 1938

Went to the swimming bath in Schoeneberg yesterday. We need to do a dive from the 3-metre board, the last of the test to earn the sports medal. I was frightened but it was not too bad.

19th February, 1938

Went with Mum to the cinema. We had to go to Berlin as we had missed 'Mutterliebe' here. It was one of the Benjamino Gigli films, we loved it; he is so good in scenes with children.

Monday, 21st February, 1938

The Führer addressed the Reichstag. He spoke for three hours, giving an account of the success of the last five years. He said he had discussions with the Austrian Chancellor and got an assurance that all the Germans in Austria are free to think and say whatever they believe without going to prison for it. We are all full of enthusiasm.

11th March, 1938

How is that possible? The same Schuschning who, only a month ago, visited the Führer on the Obersalzberg and signed an agreement, the man who set free the National Socialists in his country and spoke publicly full of admiration for the Führer and appeared to be pro-German, suddenly ill-treats the Germans. He has ordered an election for the 13th March but with very odd conditions. The voting paper allows only a 'yes'. To say 'no' one has to bring ones own piece of paper!

The German people are protesting, they demand Schuschning's resignation.

The police have been attacking people with truncheons, many have been hurt.

The election has now been postponed.

13th March, 1938

13th March, 1938

What rejoicing! Six million people wait to greet their Führer! 64 million look towards Austria with shining eyes.

Austria is German, is National Socialistic! Yesterday Schuschning resigned. The new government is asking the Führer for help. German troops are marching across the border. The Führer went to Austria, his own homeland.

One huge shout of rejoicing went through the country. The Führer spoke from Linz. Cries 'we thank our Führer', 'one nation, one country, one Führer' interrupted his address again and again. What must he have felt? One could hear the deep emotion that gripped his voice.

The Führer went on to Braunau and stood at his parents' grave and then on to Vienna.

I went to a conference in Luckenwalde. I am so happy that at a time like this I can be amongst like-minded people, share with others the feelings that move my heart.

14th March, 1938

The Führer arrived in Vienna. Ten thousands line the streets and wave after wave of joyous cries greeted the Führer when he appeared on the balcony. So much so that he had to speak to the crowds, welcoming them, his own landsmen, into the German fatherland.

It seems that Mussolini had something to do with the liberation of Austria because the Führer said "Mussolini, I will never forget!"

15th March, 1938

Today the Führer spoke from Vienna. He reported to the German nation the greatest success of his life and everywhere people rejoiced. We listened to his speech at school.

16th *March, 1938*

Another unforgettable day! It was wonderful! I got up as usual to go to school when Mum said, "You are having a day off." What better news was there? I rushed to look at the newspaper, the headline read 'The Führer is returning to Berlin at 5.00 p.m.' I knew at once : I had to be in Berlin.

Eileen was, of course, ready to go and knew of a few others who would join us.

All was easy up to the Wilhelmplatz, then the crowds thickened but we didn't intend to give up. We formed a chain, the smallest in the middle and pressed and reached the Wilhelmplatz in no time and made for the corner of Voss Strasse, right in the front row. Suddenly the SS guard of honour drew up, surely that meant the Führer's car would stop here and so it was! We heard the noise draw nearer and saw heads stretching and then the big, black car stopped just where we stood. The door was flung open and there stood the Führer! He hesitated for a moment, shook the hand of an SS officer and then walked on. I could see him very clearly – what a moment!

Then all the others followed: Goering, Goebbels, Hess, Neurath, Dr. Ley, Prince August Wilhelm.

Now everybody pressed forward to get close to the Reichskanzlei and the balcony. We lost each other, only Eileen was still with me. We too were pushing but followed the maxim – patience, politeness – and we conquered a position right under the balcony. We had to wait but the crowd tried every means of bringing the Führer to the balcony. We called 'Führer, we want to see you'. Called for Goering to bring our Führer and we sang the National Anthem.

At last he appeared, he stood just above us, looked down on us, raised his hand in greeting and I saw his eyes, very clear, steel-blue eyes.

He came again and again and we stood and gazed and joined in the jubilation.

At the station we found our lost companions and we

returned home happy and full of enthusiasm.

18th March, 1938

The Führer has just finished addressing the Reichstag. As so often he had scathing words for Mr. Eden. He also referred to Schuschning and how he broke all the promises he had made to the Führer. We are being asked to vote on 10th April, not only the Austrians, but all the German people are to give the Führer their vote of confidence. He spoke in moving words when he appealed to his people.

In Austria great changes are under way, currency, banks, the army, all will be identical to ours. The speed of the changes is fantastic. I am sure the people abroad will be most impressed.

9th April, 1938

The last day before the voting. This morning Dr. Goebbels spoke from Vienna proclaiming that today is the 'Day of Greater Germany.' Everywhere flags were hoisted and the sirens sounded. The Führer addressed the nation for the last time before voting commences and he claimed 'this country and this movement are all my work!'

End of April, 1938

Last week we celebrated Traute's confirmation. The vicar spoke very simply and it was a lovely church service.

I should have been confirmed too but Mum wanted me to wait a year so that Jurgen and I can be confirmed on the same day. I am sure it is a good idea and it will be less expensive if there is only one party.

On 26th Mum and I went to the State Opera to hear Verdi's 'Troubadore'. It was fantastic. Helge Roswaenge is my heart-throb and the applause was going on and on. Heinrich Schlussnus was also wonderful – what a voice.

I wore my long evening dress, the one I had for the wedding.

End of April, 1938

I am now going to the new school. The Gertrud Stauffacher in Mariendorf. It is only two stops further on the train for me. The School in Lichtenrade does not go on to matriculation, at least not for the girls.

Val has gone to a Secretarial College, she always wanted to be a fashion designer, but the training is long and expensive. Traute, too, is taking a secretarial course, even though she had always talked of doing something with children. I think being a secretary is for those who cannot think of anything better. I don't know what I want to be but I would hate to join the others and finish up in an office.

Mum let me continue at school, even though it cannot be easy for her when we are living on her widow's pension. Mum never allows herself any luxuries but she finds the money to pay our school fees; she gets a reduction if we are doing well.

I have three more years to do at school and I have chosen the domestic branch as it should be slightly easier, even though many of the subject we study are the same as on the scientific branch and our final examinations will be the same. The main difference is that we are spending two of the six days per week on practical work. Dressmaking, gardening or crafts, cooking and one morning at a day nursery to look after young children. Against that we take only one language, English and no Latin.

3rd May, 1938

The Führer is in Rome, he was greeted by enthusiastic crowds. The King and the Duce welcomed him at the railway station.

28th May, 1938

During our annual sport's competition Eileen presented Val and me with our confirmation as 'Schaftsführerinnen' – we wear a red and white cord.

June, 1938

Our school celebrated its 25th anniversary. Various shows were put on for the parents. One was a performance of 'Turandot' marvellously acted by the older girls. There were all kinds of stalls and the physics room was transformed into a café – it was all great fun.

July, 1938

We – Grandad, Mum, Jurgen and I – have arrived in Ruhpolding in the Bavarian Alps. The mountains here are not terribly high but it is beautiful. We are staying at a pleasant, small hotel, looking down on Ruhpolding. Grandad is only staying with us for a week but en route we stopped for a day in Munich, where he wanted to visit a distant relative. It rained all day but we saw something of Munich and in the evening we went to the famous Hofbrauhaus. Of course, it was in Munich where the Führer started his party.

Yesterday we hired a car for the day and the driver took us to Bad Reichenhall and Berchtesgarden where the Führer has his house on the Obersalzberg. Sadly, one can no longer go up to the house. From there we drove to the Konigsee. The lake is surrounded on all sides by high mountains, the sheer rock faces reaching down into the water. We had a boat trip to the other side and walked from there to the much smaller, beautiful Obersee. Then we continued into Austria and Salzburg. I was so proud to visit the country only months after its return to Germany. In Salzburg we went into a café – Austria is famous for its cafes – and when we were about to leave two young men from the neighbouring table jumped up to help me into my coat – I felt great!

*   *   *

My uncle Henry and his wife have joined us for a few days. They are on holiday in their new, dashing sports car.

They will drive up to the top of the Gross-Glockner when they leave us – very exciting for Henry. But before then they will take us on a day's outing, which will be a bit difficult because the car is really a two-seater and the three of us will have to squeeze into the spare seat at the back.

*   *   *

What a day! Mum, Jurgen and I managed to fit into the car and we set off towards Berchtesgarden. Due to the overloading, the car overheated twice. On one occasion we were quite high on a mountain and Henry and Jurgen had to climb down the mountainside to fetch water from a stream. On the return journey I saw a column of six black cars coming towards us, in my excitement I called out, "The Führer!" and there he was in the front seat of the first car. I saw him, but it all happened so quickly – I was quite overcome with emotion.

Four days later

The highest mountain near us is the Hochfelln – 1671 m. We can see it in the distance from Ruhpolding. The top is quite bare of vegetation. People here say one can walk up and back in a day. We do a lot of walking every day but that would be a tough climb.

There is a very nice gentleman in the hotel and he often talks to Mum. He reminds me a lot of my father. He offered to accompany us on our mountain expedition and Mum has agreed to it.

What a disaster of a day it turned out to be! It was a very hot day and after we had walked for an hour I think the gentleman got wet with perspiration but would not take his jacket off which made him feel worse. Somehow Jurgen and I got the devil into us. We walked very fast and were soon a long distance ahead whilst Mum must have felt that she ought to keep our guardian company. But I know she was very worried because when the path narrowed and there was a steep slope on one side and she could not see us she started calling us and we got a good telling off. But I was in a miserable state, very unsettled. I think it had something to do with overhearing my aunt saying that this gentleman seemed very interested in my Mum! The view from the summit was indescribable – snow peaks as far as we could see and the sun shining upon them. How exhilarating it is to stand on top of a mountain.

On the last evening our hostess read our hands. She told me there would be two men in my life, but when she saw Mum's hand she looked troubled and would not say what she saw.

Home Again

On our return journey we spent a night in Nuremberg in the 'Roter Hahn' hotel. We visited all the famous sights, the Dürer' House, the bridge 'Hankersteig', the fountain 'Gansemannchenbrunnen' and we saw the enormous stadium where every year the Reichsparteitag, the gathering of the Party, will take place. Most of it is still under construction but what is there is so vast, one has to imagine it filled with thousands of uniformed men and flags and banners, to understand and feel its effect. How I wish to be part of it one day.

26th August, 1938

The Hungarian Admiral v. Horthy and his wife arrived in Germany a few days ago. There was an inspection of the fleet at Kiel and the launching of a new destroyer. Yesterday he came to Berlin and there was a military parade in his honour. Val and I went to see it, we found a good place. The Charlotten Chaucee has been widened this year and the foundation for the Victory Column is being constructed. When the Führer returned with Admiral Horthy he drove very slowly and we saw him quite near to us.

September, 1938

We are going to have our own house built. Henry will design it as he is an architect now. He works in Berlin and has a lot of contacts. My mother will have to take out a big mortgage, but I think it was my father's ambition to own a house. I have seen the plot of land, it is just a piece of waste ground. Ours will be the only one in this short road, which is no more than a lane of grass and mud. The ten minutes walk from the railway station will be rather a lonely one along a dark, unmade road. My grandfather will do all the excavation work himself. As the house is to have cellars (a storage room, tool room, washroom and the now obligatory air-raid shelter) he will have to dig at least one metre deep.

10th September, 1938

The Reichsparteitag 'Greater Germany' is now in progress in Nuremberg. I wish I could be there. The Führer addressed the German Youth today. He spoke very movingly. It really frightened me when he said, "One day, when destiny calls me away from my people, there will be another leader … …"

Traute and I have enrolled for ballroom dancing lessons – Mr. Ganschow seems to be a gentleman of the old school.

14th September, 1938

On Monday we heard another wonderful speech by the Führer, one that was eagerly awaited abroad. He said that the position of the Sudeten Germans would have to be improved or we would offer them our help. Prague replied by imposing a curfew on several towns. Thirteen people have died in three days. Konrad Henlein, the leader of the Sudeten Germans, demanded that the curfew was lifted and the military withdrawn within the next six hours – this was not done. Henlein has now broken off negotiations. We are almost prepared for a war declaration – may God deliver us from that! Even though Germany is economically secure for some years and even though enormous defence installations in the West will be ready by the end of the year, nothing worse could happen to us now.

The latest news is that Chamberlain is coming to meet the Führer.

15th September, 1938
Went to the Deutsche Opera to hear 'Euryanthe'.

17th September, 1938
Chamberlain went to the Obersalzberg to meet the Führer. He returned to London this afternoon but will come back again.

A warrant has been issued for Henlein because in a proclamation he declared that the Sudeten Germans want to return to their homeland. 15,000 people have already fled, mostly men who were being forced into the Czech army.

19th September, 1938
I think war is almost inevitable because Chamberlain consulted with the French President Daladier and the whole world believes there should be a referendum in Czechoslovakia, but the Czechs said they would never agree to that. 84,000 Germans have now fled. The Sudeten Party has been prohibited. Henlein formed a freedom corps and 40,000 men have already enlisted.

The Duce spoke yesterday. He supported the idea of a referendum but if not he expressed the hope that a war would be restricted to one between Germany and Czechoslovakia. If even that is not possible Italy would fight on Germany's side.

24th September, 1938
Chamberlain has been back to Germany and consulted with the Führer in Bad Godesberg in order to preserve peace, but war is looming. The Czech government has

resigned and has been replaced by a military government. Prague is mobilising. Henlein issued a proclamation calling on all Sudeten Germans to ignore these orders. There were again many dead. Apparently, preparations are being made to blow up all strategic points in case of our troops entering the country. We expect the Czechs will receive our memorandum today, a last attempt to achieve a peaceful solution.

25th September, 1938

My grandfather's birthday. The whole family assembled, everybody talks as if war was a certainty.

The Duce spoke, saying that Italy is ready for war. The Czech have to decide by 1st October.

Wednesday, 28th September, 1938

All the heads of State – from Italy, France and Great Britain – are meeting the Führer in Munich.

At home we have arguments every day. My mother and Aunt Anna are accusing me of wanting a war.

30th September, 1938

Negotiations went on into the night at Munich and what a wonderful agreement they reached! Tomorrow our troops will march into Czechoslovakia and occupy all the German territories. We thank God for preserving peace and blessing the Führer's work

1st October, 1938

The Führer will be in Berlin today. Eileen came at 7.00 a.m. to collect me, but Mum would not let me go, as we were supposed to be at school. Fortunately, the school closed after an hour and I went with the others to the Wilhelmplatz. We saw the Führer arrive, he looked very happy – we stayed on to shout and sing, there was so much rejoicing!

13th October, 1938

The Führer is visiting the liberated Sudetenland, the scenes were indescribable – our soldiers are receiving an enormous welcome.

16th October, 1938

We are now going to our dancing classes. It is quite fun, especially as there are usually more boys than girls, but they are all rather stupid.

9th December, 1938

On the 1st November, our Ambassador in Paris was shot by a Jew and he died on the 9th.

The Jews in Germany are having a bad time now. They have to pay 6 billion Marks, are not allowed to own weapons and are excluded from many professions. Some Jewish shops had their windows smashed. This is getting us a bad name.

In January I will be working for a month in the Pestalozzi-Fröbel house, looking after babies. This is a day nursery for children and is world-famous. It is part of our school training, all directed at preparing us for being good housewives and mothers. The following year we should spend a month on a large farm or country house – it will be a change from going to school – but I am not very good at these practical jobs. When we have our cooking lessons I rather do the menial tasks and leave the complicated ones to others. Worst are the days when we go to the day nursery. I hate being given a group of small children and told to play certain games with them, especially now that we have to keep indoors.

The year ended rather well, aunt Lisa took me to the State Opera – she gets tickets regularly every month – we heard 'Tannhäuser'. It was fantastic. Set Swanholm is now another of my heart-throbs. He sang and acted with such passion – unforgettable!

15th January, 1939

Our ball was held in Teltow last night – the crowning glory of our dancing classes. Traute and I had no special partners, so we sat with our family. Our grandfather and an aunt and uncle had come to witness our 'great day'! Eileen made her excuses, she is now otherwise interested.

Pestalozzi-Fröbel House – 29th January, 1939

Working here is very good even though I manage to get so many things wrong.

Yesterday I had to bathe a baby only four months old, I was scared. We all love little Manfred, he is not quite a year old but with his charm and smile he has all of us dancing attention. Before the mothers come in the evening to collect their children we have to dress the babies and generally get them ready, but we are not allowed to hand them over until Sister has approved – of course, I forget – another telling off! We have been right through all the jobs from washing nappies and scrubbing potties, to preparing bottles and the baby food.

Another week and we shall be back at school – how awful!

February, 1939

Our confirmation will be on 2nd April. Jurgen and I have been going to confirmation classes, once a week, since last year. Our Vicar is quite jolly and not so very concerned with religion. Sometimes he discusses football with the boys. He told us that he went into the Church because it was the only way to get into College without paying a fee. He is a very good preacher, the church is full every Sunday.

The great news is that Uncle Werner and his family are returning to Germany for good. They went to Brazil some years ago to escape the miserable conditions here. My uncle looked after some big engineering jobs in Brazil.

We expect the war in Spain to be over soon, General

Franco took Barcelona.

15th March, 1939

The Czechs are growing very impertinent. First they had it in for the Slovaks and then the Germans. Many people have been wounded in fighting.

Last night our troops marched into Bohemia, they will be there as protectors for the population against the Bolshevic hordes. It all seems very wonderful – another success.

16th March, 1939

My uncle and his family are arriving from Brazil tomorrow. Unfortunately I shall not be at home. We are taking our girls on a Youth Hostel weekend from 18-19th and I cannot let Eileen down.

22nd March, 1939

Another wonderful success. Lithuania has returned the Memelland to us. We are so used to these successes that many people hardly took any notice.

On Sunday the Führer returned from his visit to Bohemia. It was a triumphal arrival in Berlin. Unfortunately I could not be there. My uncle visited us, his first since his return. My cousin has changed so much. She used to be such a baby. She was always too young for us to play with her. Now, I think she will want to join the Hitler Youth, if they stay here.

4th April, 1939

Our confirmation went very well. Mum made me a black – one has to wear black – velvet dress and all our relatives came to the church. I had a bit of a disagreement with the Vicar a few weeks prior to this Sunday. It is customary for the Vicar to choose a quotation from the Bible for every person confirmed into the Church, as a kind of guide throughout life. But our Vicar asked us to select our own word from the Bible. In our village church the gallery is decorated with sayings from the Bible and in the centre are written the words: "One God, One Nation, One Führer," so I chose that, but the Vicar refused, as it was not a quotation from the Bible. My reply was that he should find one for me himself.

We were 20 people for lunch on that day – just the number we can seat around our dinner table – and we had lots of presents – I love the opera glasses that Mum gave me.

10th April, 1939

We had our history essays back, mine was the best. I love history lessons, especially as we no longer have to memorise dates but look at whole periods of history and see the connections with other countries and epochs. I am not very good at math or science and music is awful, having to stand up and sing!

In France and England there are outcries because we incorporated Czechoslovakia into the Greater Germany. They speculate that by 1941 we shall have taken Scandinavia, Rumania, Hungary, Belgium and France and whatever else! Well, I suppose they know!

1st July, 1939

We are celebrating 'Richtefest' at our new house. The building is complete except for the roof tiles. We have to treat the bricklayers to celebrate completion of their work. Mum will provide beer and Frankfurters with potato salad.

Val is in charge of the 'Gruppe' in Blankenfelde now, I shall be taking over Mahlow because Eileen has been promoted. I went on a 2-week training course in Ossig in June. Christel, the girl in charge, was so good, a beautiful girl and full of enthusiasm.

22ⁿᵈ August, 1939

I no longer think that there will be a war. Germany has signed a non-aggression pact with Russia, a surprise to everybody and the British have tried for weeks, or months, to humour the Russians – poor Mr. Chamberlain!

Monday, 28ᵗʰ August, 1939

Though we were not officially told, but mobilisation is in progress. Everybody who was told to report on the first day of mobilisation was called up on Saturday. As from today all food, except bread, potatoes, fruit and vegetables is only available on ration coupons.

Three anti-aircraft guns appeared in the fields around our village.

On Sunday Eileen and I met at 6.00 a.m. We cycled from house to house to gather all our 13 and 14 year old girls to report at 8.00 a.m. for a day helping with the harvest. We had a lovely time, building a large haystack.

The Reichsparteitag in Nuremberg has been cancelled – Eileen was due to attend!

Thursday, 31ˢᵗ August, 1939

The British Government has offered to mediate. The Führer has made a fabulous offer to the Poles. Danzig is to return to Germany with immediate effect, the future of the Polish Corridor will be settled by a referendum in which every person resident in the area on 1ˢᵗ January, 1938 will be eligible to vote. The Poles were given until 12 noon to send a negotiator, but nobody came. The uncertainty is hard to bear. We now wear our uniform to school.

FIRST WAR YEAR

(Translated from my diary)

1ˢᵗ September, 1939. Morning

The Führer has called on our troops. Force must be met with force. There has already been fighting at the Radio Station Gleiwitz.

The school has given us a day off – Danzig declared itself to be German. We hope England will not interfere.

Same day. 2.00 p.m.

The Führer spoke at 10.00 a.m. He said from now on he will wear his beloved grey (army) uniform and he will only part with it again when peace has been restored, or not at all. If he should not survive, Hermann Goring will be his successor and after him it will be Rudolf Hess.

I cannot visualise a time when there is no Adolf Hitler.

The German troops opened fire at 5.45. p.m. Our armies are lined up along the whole of the Polish border. German aircraft attacked several towns but only military objects. The Führer said he did not wish to fight a war against defenceless women and children. He added that he knew that the German youth was ready, with pride in their eyes, to serve the nation.

The Polish newspapers have declared that our offer is ridiculous.

Saturday, 2ⁿᵈ September, 1939

Our troops are on the move. From East Prussia they are moving West. The others are going East and they have already split Poland into two parts.

The Peninsula Hela has been attacked from the sea. Our bombers had a go at Posen, Lodz, Warsaw, Gdingen and others.

Last night we had the first air raid alarm at 7.00 p.m. Nobody went into the shelter – it was over after five minutes.

England still has not made a decision. I don't think the Führer wants war with England. We have always been taught that the British people are our kinsmen.

3ʳᵈ *September, 1939*

The world has gone mad!!

England sent an ultimatum. They consider themselves at war with us unless we undertake by 11.00 a.m. to withdraw our troops from Polish territory.

The Führer said yesterday that the fighting in Poland will be over within a few weeks but then he spoke of the coming months and years – I am sure a war against England would last years – we cannot get at them on their island.

4ᵗʰ *September, 1939*

When the moment came that we knew we were at war with England – and France – I was standing by the window, looking out into the garden. I felt no elation, only a dull foreboding.

7ᵗʰ *September, 1939*

Some British bombers came across, but they have all been turned back.

9ᵗʰ *September, 1939*

Our tanks moved into Warsaw. British aircraft dropped propaganda leaflets yesterday.

There has been the first skirmish between the French and our troops. The French came across our border – after Göring had said that we would not commence the fighting as we had no quarrel with them.

Henry's wife has been told that she has to work in the factory in Schonefeld. All young women who have no children have to work.

14th September, 1939

14th September, 1939

Canada has declared war on us.

We expect Russia to join into the war any day. They want to grab the parts of Poland which they wish to acquire. Lots of their young men have been called up and sent to the frontier.

Our school certificate has been up-graded. It will give us the same entitlement as the one from the scientific branch.

19th September, 1939

The Führer visited Danzig today.

We now have to go to school in the afternoon, very strange!

21st September, 1939

The war in Poland is nearly over. Only in Warsaw and Hela the resistance has not quite been overcome.

Nothing happens on the Western front.

Saturday, 23rd September, 1939

Eileen got engaged. Her fiancé is likely to be posted to Poland any day; they went to buy the rings today.

29th September, 1939

Warsaw has capitulated, only on the Peninsula Hela the fighting continues. Ribbentrop went again to Moscow, an agreement was signed yesterday. A great exchange in goods is provided for. We shall work together for peace or Russia will be our ally. Poor England!

The Führer visited Wilhelmshafen and the U-boats. Two British aircraft carriers have already been destroyed.

It was fun at school today, nobody would believe Eileen's engagement! I had top marks again for a history essay.

2nd October, 1939

Our troops marched into Warsaw and Hela capitulated, thus the war in Poland is over.

Jurgen has gone off today. A workforce has been organised to bring in the harvest.

Sunday, 8th October, 1939

We arrived in Shaffelde three days ago. There are fifteen of us to help with the harvest. The Hitler Youth is organising this work. Eileen is in charge of our group and she has to conduct some meetings in the evenings.

We are distributed to farms around the village and shall live with the families and work with them. Eileen and I are, unfortunately, left with a family in a neighbouring village as in our family one of the children has measles.

We had a terrible day on Friday. The weather was cold and wet and we were kneeling all day on a small sack of straw digging up the potatoes and gathering them into baskets. One expected us to keep up with the farm workers, which is not easy. We start early in the morning and finish at about 7.00 p.m. It seems rain is no reason for stopping work. But however hard, I must stick it for the six weeks we are supposed to do this work.

Eileen received news that she is to return home. Head Office want her for other work and early this morning her fiancé came to fetch her. I feel so depressed I nearly cried! - and on Monday I have to move to the other family.

Tuesday, 10th October, 1939

My new family is very nice. A school teacher is working alongside me. We talk all the time, discussing quite profound subjects. Two soldiers arrived today. They were called up recently but the army cannot use them yet, so they were told to help on the farms. Work is much easier now.

Thursday, 12th October, 1939

The maize we were harvesting today was full of nettles and we got stung mercilessly. Otherwise I am very happy here. Everybody is so nice, including the two soldiers, one in particular: we are having a lot of fun together.

Food is something that takes a bit of getting used to. Lunch is brought out to us. One of the farm workers comes out with a dog-drawn cart. We all sit down by the side of the field – no chance to wash ones hands – and eat. The evening meal, too, was a bit unexpected. The whole family, farm workers and all, sit around the table, in the centre of which are two large bowls, one containing potatoes, the other cottage cheese or a gravy. We all dip our potatoes into the second bowl and that is it.

Going to the loo is the other problem when we are working. There isn't a tree or bush in sight. So one squats behind the wagon that collects the potatoes and hopes everybody is looking the other way.

Saturday, 14th October, 1939

What shall I do? Our soldiers asked me to a dance. I would love to go but I have nothing to wear, only my working clothes and my uniform. Besides, we are not supposed to go dancing.

Sunday, 15th October, 1939

We worked very hard today. All the farmer's relatives from Berlin came. A machine dug up the potatoes, what we had to do was collect them into baskets and then unload them into the wagon. The Berliners would not believe that I was not from the village. They were full of praise- I enjoyed it.

Wednesday, 18th October, 1939

Mum sent a parcel with a decent dress.

Our soldiers are leaving tomorrow and there will be a

farewell dance. I hope they won't mind if I don't go. (I would like to though.) I get on so well with Werner. At first we just joked and teased, but during the last few days we had quite serious discussions. He took to calling me 'Ingelein', in the beginning it was 'Fräulein Inge'. Both the soldiers said I was the only bright spot, without me they would have perished! It is a pity it is coming to an end.

20th October, 1939

Our soldiers are staying on until Tuesday. I am so glad I am not left alone here. We had our farewell dance all the same and I went!! I danced with Werner most of the time.

24th October, 1939

They have left this morning! I am not very good at saying 'good-bye', in fact I dreaded it. But they went so early, I was still asleep. Not a parting word! But they left me a charming letter.

Ribbentrop spoke in Danzig. He said that England had refused the Führer's peace offer and that we would now put all our energies into the continuing war effort.

Sunday, 29th October, 1939

Mum and Jurgen came today to visit me. I found out too late that the family here is celebrating the baby's christening. But they did not mind, there was plenty of food; we have not had such a good meal for a long time. I was so glad for Mum.

The same evening I learnt that we are returning home on Tuesday. The school will no longer tolerate our absence – silly!

Thursday, 9th November, 1939

The Führer has been saved by a miracle! He was in Munich to commemorate the day when the first of his followers died in his cause. He addressed his old comrades in the Bürgerbräu cellar but left earlier than planned to hurry back to Berlin. No sooner had he gone when a bomb exploded. My knees were shaking when Mum told me. Who could do such a thing? How could we have carried on without him? Seven people were killed and sixty-three injured.

We shall be moving into our new house on Tuesday.

16th November, 1939

We have already been here for 10 days. It is very nice and comfortable. Mum has a proper gas cooker – we had the house specially connected to the gas mains from the next road as Mum would not change to cooking electric.

Our aircraft are making daily flights over France and England. Four British warships have been badly damaged by our bombs.

29th November, 1939

British warships went down off the coast of Ireland and the Scottish Isles. I don't think England can last long now. We hear of many skirmishes at the Finnish-Russian Border.

18th December, 1939

We have a funny situation now. Eileen is engaged to her opposite number in the youth movement. Christa seems to spend a lot of time with her opposite number and now the others want to link me to Ulli. We often walk home together as he lives very near to us. But I am so glad the planned pre-Christmas party has been cancelled. Eileen asked me whether she should place Ulli or Rudi next to me at the table. I chose Ulli but only because I would not admit that I prefer Rudi by far.

We organised a children's afternoon for last week. Seventy children came. Christa had prepared a Punch and Judy show. It was lovely.

Two days later we had a parents' evening with a lot of

talking – all went well and it was a great success.

At the weekend another collection for the Winter Aid Fund was due. December is, by tradition, the Hitler Youth's turn to take the collection boxes around. We did very well, over 100.00 DM in Mahlow alone. We are quite skilled now, we go into shops and travel on trains where people cannot escape us.

On Thursday our 'Graf Spee' was involved in a gun battle off Monte Video with three British warships, all of which sustained heavy damage. Our ship went into the harbour. To our horror we hear today that the Führer ordered Captain Longsdorf to sink the 'Graf Spee' as Uruguay refused entry into the harbour and on leaving again she would have fallen into enemy hands.

But England is suffering heavy losses in the air. Of forty-four bombers approaching Germany, thirty-four were shot down.

24th December, 1939
War-time Christmas.

Christmas Eve has been and gone and I hardly noticed it. What a wonderful time Christmas used to be! The Advent weeks full of preparations and secrecy and then the moment when the door opened and there was the magic of Christmas, the tree and twenty-four candles spreading a warm light around the room and presents waiting to be joyfully received – and now the magic has gone. Being in a new house does not help, all traditions have been disturbed.

The family will still come, but the feeling is different.

New Year's Day 1940
A new year – will it bring peace? Whatever, the German people will prove strong. May the Führer have faithful friends by his side – I wish I could do more to help.

2nd *February, 1940*

It is a terribly cold winter this year. Down to -20°C. We have a few days relief and then it is down again. We go to school for only an hour to collect a lot of homework, but it is very cold at home too. The wall behind my bed glistens with ice every morning – the house hasn't had time to dry out. We are short of fuel, it has to be collected from the Coal Merchant but we are only allocated one hundred-weight at a time and, to make it worse, we cannot buy the special fuel we need for our hot-air heating system – our poor soldiers!

One of the girls at school got hold of addresses of soldiers who want to correspond with young girls. I now have an address.

18th *February, 1940*

This is a terrible winter. Even the older people cannot remember a winter as cold as this. It started just after Christmas – the temperatures hover between -10° and -20°C. today it was -20°C at 8.00 a.m. and must have been lower during the night.

And now the snow! It has been snowing for 48 hours. I have been out shovelling snow twice a day to keep a path open to the nearest road. The Hitler Youth was called out to clear the railway station and its approaches. In Berlin the Jews have to do the snow clearing. It is piled up a metre high in the streets. What a problem it will be when the thaw sets in!

We are still short of solid fuel. The schools can no longer be heated. We go in three times a week for just twenty minutes or so and take work home – where it is also cold, so cold.

A rumour has it that our final examinations will be brought forward to October. That will be impossible; we have lost so much time with the potato harvest and now this freeze. Even without this, our teachers are frightening us by saying that we are not keeping up with the curriculum and shall never pass the examinations.

23rd February, 1940

How the weather has changed. Two days ago –15°, yesterday 17° at midday. We had planned to go skiing, but the thaw put an end to it. We enjoyed half an hour sunbathing instead!

But our water pump is frozen. Perhaps it was not such a good idea to save money by relying on our own water supply, pumping it up from underground sources. We have to walk down the road to the Nursery and collect two buckets of water at a time.

Had the first meeting today with my new 'Schaft', I had to hold it in our house, we cannot heat our normal meeting place.

1st March, 1940

Our U-boats are having great successes. The Führer decorated Herbert Schulze with the Great Cross of the Iron Cross.

The thaw is dreadful, our garden is one large lake. The farmers have lost all the potatoes in the severe frost.

16th March, 1940

Well, the British thought they could support Finland against Russia and spread the war. But they miscalculated, Russia and Finland signed a peace pact – Russia gaining a few islands.

17th March, 1940

Our bombers have attacked – and badly damaged – four British warships in Scapa Flow.

'Eintopfsonntag'. Once a month, in the winter, we are all asked to eat a simple stew for our dinner and give to the collection for the poor all the money we save. Today our anti-aircraft units cooked for the local population. We gathered at one of the pubs and ate our pea soup – with lots of meat and without meat coupons!

18th March, 1940

The Führer met the Duce at the Brenner.

I now have another address of a soldier to whom I shall write – I hope he will reply soon.

26th March, 1940

Nothing much happens at the front. My soldier has replied. He is only 19 years old, he serves in an airborne unit attached to the Navy.

8th April, 1940

The Norwegians are laying minefields off the coast.

We now go to school in the afternoon, from 2.00 p.m. to 7.00 p.m. Just another difficulty! Our cooking lessons are much hampered. The School no longer receives extra coupons. We should be tackling the more elaborate dishes. For the final examination we should be able to prepare a four-course dinner. In dressmaking too we started with children's clothes but our next item is a cocktail dress. We hope to be allocated extra coupons for the material.

9th April, 1940

What a day! At 12 noon I turned on the radio and heard military music – I waited for the special announcement. It came but what an announcement! At 5.00 a.m. this morning our troops marched into Denmark. Copenhagen has been occupied. The Führer ordered this to preserve the peace in the North. England intended to act within the next few days to occupy the whole of Scandinavia and wage war against us from the North. We don't want a war in the North, we will keep the countries occupied until the war is over. Denmark has agreed to it, Norway will have to!

Our bombers were again over Scapa Flow. It is said that in Berlin people embraced each other in the streets.

10th April, 1940

Everything progresses to plan in Norway and Denmark. Only ten hours and the British would have landed there first. We did a lot of damage to their troop transport fleet. Eleven of their boats have been badly damaged. Unfortunately, our 'Blücher' and 'Karlsruhe' went down. Most of the crews were saved.

11th April, 1940

Churchill is admitting the heavy losses his Navy has suffered. The occupation of Norway is progressing, some resistance is being encountered.

I assume 'my' soldier will be in Denmark. He is on the battleship 'Nuremberg'.

Eileen's father has been called up, her fiancé hopes to go to the front soon – poor Eileen.

13th April, 1940

Two British U-boats have been destroyed today.

There are sea battles fought along the Norwegian coast.

16th April, 1940

Another British battleship has gone down – the radio keeps playing the 'England' song.

But there is heavy fighting at Narvik, our destroyers against their battleships,

30th April, 1940

Contact has been established between Trontheim and Oslo. Not much England can do now! The Führer thanked the soldiers in Norway.

5th May, 1940

The British troops are fleeing from Norway. We are

bombarding their ships – they cannot have many left.

7th May, 1940

My grandfather has really made a good job of our garden. Steps lead down from the terrace to the lawn. There is a small pond and flower borders all around the fence. In one corner Mum has a little vegetable plot framed by redcurrant and gooseberry bushes. We had to laugh at my grandfather: he planted cherry, pear and plum trees but no apples – he cannot eat apples!

10th May, 1940

At 5.00 a.m. our troops marched into Holland, Belgium and Luxembourg – the British were going to occupy them to have a base for the attack on our Ruhr area. All their plans were depending on this. Too bad, they came too late. Holland declared war on us. In reply our aircraft bombed British and French harbours. I suppose now the real war will commence.

11th May, 1940

Our troops are advancing in the West. A thousand prisoners were taken. We are bombing French airfields.

13th May, 1940

This morning Luttich fell into our hands. About a thousand aircraft were destroyed in the last three days. Our boys are truly wonderful.

15th May, 1940

What a time we live in! Rotterdam has capitulated, soon afterwards the Dutch government followed suit. Queen Wilhelmina is in London. Many more aircraft were shot down. The first tank battle took place near Namur. The French were beaten, chased by our air force. The Maginot line was breached.

16th May, 1940

Our boys opened a gap a hundred kilometres wide through the Maginot line. One special announcement chases the next on the radio. The Belgian Government fled to Ostende, our forces reached Brussels. The war will soon be over.

19th May, 1940

Our troops are moving deep into France. The government is preparing to flee to Bordeaux.

One of our neighbours returned from Freiburg which suffered a heavy air attack. Fifty people died during the first attack alone.

21st May, 1940

One gigantic battle! The French army which formed the link between Belgium and the Maginot line has been destroyed and a wide door opened for our troops to flood into France. The French seem to become very uneasy. The British troops are retiring towards home.

And with all this happening I am supposed to think of what I want to do when I leave school next year! Mum suggested a teacher training, there are 1-year courses available now but I cannot see myself as a teacher. Authority does not come easily to me (despite all my experience in the Hitler Youth.) I thought of librarian, but this demands a long training and I cannot expect my mother to keep me for much longer. One can do the training through practical work but that would make me little more than a shop assistant.

27th May, 1940

Calais capitulated yesterday. We are sending parachute troops and Alpine regiments to Narvik, the situation there does not look very good.

28ᵗʰ May, 1940

We were in the middle of our cooking lessons when one of the girls rushed in – 'Belgium has capitulated!' We were beside ourselves with joy. King Leopold will be treated with all honours, his troops fought manfully.

2ⁿᵈ June, 1940

The British who vanished so quickly from France are now talking of a long-anticipated and planned retreat!

We all expect Italy to join into the war any day now. The real war against England will commence now.

Two of our Heinkel 109 aircraft collided near here. Eight men died. Pieces of metal are scattered over a large area.

5ᵗʰ June, 1940

The battle of Flanders is over – 10,000 died on our side – 10,000! Dunkirk was taken – a terrible defeat for the British. Some sad survivors reached home. Our march into France continues.

10ᵗʰ June, 1940

Another page of world history has been written. Narvik is ours at last. The British withdrew, Norway capitulated.

For two months our heroes there held out, now they are free – we are so happy for them.

Another news flash! The Duce will speak at 6.00 p.m. We all guessed what was coming. With enormous applause the Duce declared that from tomorrow the Italian soldiers will fight side by side against the Western powers with us.

12ᵗʰ June, 1940

Malta has been bombarded. Canada declared war on Italy.

I have a problem. I am not coping with responsibilities with the Group, at least, not with the leaders under me.

Shall I resign? No!

14th June, 1940
Paris capitulated.
We almost fell into each others' arms at school when the news came through. Handed over without a fight! Our troops are marching into the town! Other towns are tumbling. France won't last long now!

17th June, 1940
France has laid down the weapons! We cannot believe it! No more fighting in the West! Last night Petain took over the government in France and today he surrendered.
At school we were in the middle of a physics paper when we were called into the assembly hall. News from the front? Or something to do with the school? The Head Master said 'A special announcement of great political and military importance is expected.' We guessed but could not believe it. The fanfares sounded, there was a dead silence in the hall, we hardly dared to breathe and then 'Petain has asked for a truce.' A great cry echoed through the hall. On the way home in the train people smiled at us when we told them the news. And what did I do when I got home? I started sewing my blouse and prepared the beans for bottling! Cruel, maddening on such a day.

21st June, 1940
The longest day, the sun is turning and history is being reversed! In the Forest of Compiegne, at the very same spot, in the same railway coach, where 22 years ago Germany's defeat was sealed, the Führer is meeting the French delegation – we have wiped out the humiliation of 1918. But will it mean peace? Probably not.

24th June, 1940
The air raid sirens sounded during the night. I slept

through it. Only Mum was awake. The Post Office in Babelsberg is burning.

25th June, 1940

Twenty minutes ago peace was restored in the West – one can hardly grasp the idea.

27th June, 1940

We are writing a history essay. Subject: 25th June, 1940. My soldier has written from Denmark.

4th July, 1940

We are on school holidays for seven weeks but I have been offered a holiday job for three weeks, as an assistant in a holiday play group in Treptow – I hope it will be all right!

The Italian Marshall Balbo was killed in an aircraft accident.

We saw all the latest events in the cinema – it was wonderful.

8th July, 1940

I like my job at Treptow, the children are nice.

21st August, 1940

The Italians took British Somaliland yesterday. The British evacuated their troops and made a strategic withdrawal.

Our aircraft are very busy over England, a hundred aircraft shot down every day.

26th August, 1940

Woke up at 1.00 a.m. last night. There was a lot of rumbling and noise in the air – a storm! But then it did not quite sound like a storm. I realised the anti-aircraft guns were in action. At that moment Mum came to wake us. We watched from the window the bright flashes of the guns and the flares illuminating the sky. Then there was the sound of aircraft overhead. We retired to the cellar. Grandad insisted on going up into the loft to have a better view of events. Once, it sounded as if the guns were outside the house, the windows and doors rattled. After half an hour all was quiet, we went back to bed, but then the shooting started again. Off to the cellar again. We waited and in the end returned to bed – our sirens had failed! We heard that bombs fell a few kilometres away. One person was killed, one aircraft came down.

28ᵗʰ August, 1940

I went with Mum to Berlin. The school provided us with coupons to buy dress material for our 'masterpiece'. We are to make a cocktail dress or something like it. We always do our shopping at Wertheim at the Potsdamer Platz. The store is not very exciting now but when we were children Mum took us there for her Christmas shopping. There was a fairyland in the big hall, a wonderful show for the children with a Father Christmas and animals and fairies and toys and snow and all of it moving. It was the beginning of the wonder that was Christmas. And we always finished in the cafe where we were allowed to chose a piece of gateau with lots of cream whilst Mum had her coffee – happy, happy childhood!

This time I only bought my length of dress material and I think I made a mistake. I came home with a very flimsy material, the red flower motif had caught my eyes – but it will be so difficult to sew that I shall probably make a mess of it – how stupid!

1ˢᵗ September, 1940

One year of war!

We have had four air raids and the guns around here have been firing. They come almost every night now. We spend hours in the air-raid shelter. I have started doing my school homework there. If the raids are very long we are allowed to arrive two hours later at school.

People are becoming very disgruntled. They complain about everything and nothing. We are collecting shrapnel from the anti-aircraft guns every day. The enemy aircraft usually drop flares that illuminate the countryside, one floated right above our house.

4th September, 1940 – 3.30 a.m.

We just left the air-raid shelter. Two and a half hours we spent there. A lot of bombing went on all around us. The anti-aircraft guns are now stationed in the gravel pit not far away from us.

Late September, 1940

Nothing happens on the front which now stretches from the Arctic Circle to the Mediterranean. How are we going to man this enormous stretch of frontier? The bombing of Berlin and our industry is worrying and tears on our nerves.

It does not help us at school. I think the teachers are as nervous as we are. Shall I be able to cope with the examinations in a few months' time? I am not much good at the practical tasks – dressmaking, cooking, child-care, math, physics, chemistry are no strong subject of mine. I cope as we go along, but if the exam. papers go back to something we learnt a year ago I shall be sunk! In sport I could cope only with anything that involves throwing. Nobody ever wants me when it comes to team sport. In indoors sport I am awful. I hang like a sack of potatoes on any piece of equipment. Music is hopeless. If they taught us music history or explained what a symphony is! But standing up and singing? In English I might get by. So that just leaves history and literature for me!

Early October, 1940

My aunt, Mum's sister, has been detailed to work in a

factory in Schonefeld. She has never been out to work before. Mum won't have to as she has my grandfather to look after, but she is now distributing the ration cards once a month. Her district is the village which is quite good. It is not far to walk and we know most of the farmers, they are either my mother's contemporaries or Jurgen and I went to school with their children. I think Mum will be able to get a hundred-weight of potatoes or carrots, it will help us through the winter.

I have decided I must stay on at school to the end – two girls in my class have left, they were so discouraged. Mum has made too many sacrifices to give us a good education. She never allows herself any pleasures. When I think of it a few years ago, when Benjamino Gigli sang at the Deutsche Opera, she so much wanted to hear him – we had seen all his films – but the seats were 25.00 DM – an enormous price, and she did not go! I wish she had.

29th October, 1940

We have air-raids almost every night. Sometimes we spend the whole night in the cellar. Last night bombs fell in the field opposite us, one only fifty metres from the house.

I had a big surprise last week. I came home late from school and found my soldier, Eric, waiting for me. He is on home leave. I think he and Mum got on very well, but we ran out of conversation after a short time.

The Berliner schools are going to be evacuated. Some of the Hitler Youth leaders are going with the schools to help run the camps. Two girls in my class have already gone. It is not certain whether Eileen and I are going, we don't live in Berlin. If we are allowed to join, we shall receive our school certificates without sitting the examinations! That will be a relief!

Rudi has volunteered for military service. The boys are so keen to join, they fear the war may be over before they had a chance to do their bit.

The Führer was in Florence a few days ago. He met General Franco and Petain.

Her ends the diary I kept, except for a few pages covering 1944.

EVACUATION

(i)   Jurata

November, 1940

Hurrah, I am going!

It has been agreed somewhere that, though I don't live in Berlin and don't belong to the Hitler Youth in Berlin, I can go to assist in running the evacuation camps of the Berliner schools. Only the 10-14 year old children will go with their teachers. I think we are to share responsibility with the teachers. I only have a few days to get ready. I dread the 'good-bye', I am as upset as Mum is.

Jurata, Mid-November, 1940

We have arrived in Jurata on the peninsula Hela – a year ago they were fighting here. I looked to find it on a map before we left. It is a narrow strip of land, 20 km long with the town of Hela at the very tip of it. In places it cannot be wider than half a kilometre. To the north stretches the Baltic Sea, to he south one should be able to see the coast of East Prussia across the Haff.

We set off from Berlin in the afternoon; hundreds of children and their parents milling around the station platform. Somehow the children were sorted into the compartments according to their destination.

I felt rather lost, not knowing anybody apart from Eileen, who had disappeared to the other end of the train.

As we tried to settle down for the night I passed a girl of my age in the corridor, we looked at each other and stopped for a moment. I liked her, she had a strong, intelligent face, her hair straight back – like mine – tied into a bun at the back of her neck. She said her name was Linda.

The following morning we changed trains in Danzig, a big sorting out took place as every school went off to a different location. We took about two hundred children, from three schools, to Jurata. The railway station here is minute, just a couple of what might be called platforms and right above them towers our new home, the Hotel 'Lido'.

Three Days Later

We are beginning to find our feet! Linda is here too, which is very comforting for me. She never was a Hitler Youth leader. We share a room with another girl, a couple of years younger. There are two other girls, Eve and Bridget. Eve is a born leader and has already taken command. It is evident that the teachers, who were sent by their school, have no intention of doing more than the teaching of their subjects. After which they disappear from sight and we take over.

The children are quite nicely accommodated three or four to a room. It seems a miracle how this hotel, which has obviously stood empty since the fighting here, has been equipped with all the furniture, bedding and all that the kitchen needs in such a short time. We must explore our surroundings!

One Week Later

What a place Jurata is! Apparently, it used to be the seaside resort for the rich Poles.

Our first walk was to the sea. It is only a hundred metres or so, up over the dunes and there, below, is the Baltic. A calm sea stretching away to the horizon. To the right and the left the beach is pure and undisturbed. We turned right along the white sand because at a short distance loomed a large building, all isolated and perched on top of the dunes. We found it to be derelict, the windows broken but most of the interior still intact – it used to be the casino.

The centre of the peninsula around here is wooded and amongst the pine trees we discovered bungalows, all empty and neglected. The weekend hide-outs of the privileged.

The next day we inspected the southern side of the

peninsula. Almost hidden from sight by trees and rushes appeared the Haff, the stretch of water separating us from the mainland.

Barbara, a girl of our age, has been seconded to assist here. She comes from a village near Danzig. I think we shall get on well with her.

December, 1940

We have now settled into a routine, which keeps us very busy. We start the day with a short ceremony hoisting the flag. After breakfast the teachers take over and we prepare and gather our thoughts for the afternoon programme. Eve makes all the decisions and we conduct the afternoon meetings in the way we used to conduct our weekly Hitler Youth gatherings. We mix talks and discussions with singing and reading. After lunch the children have time for the homework and one hour free time.

We keep an eye on the tidiness of the rooms, the children's clothes and their general welfare. It is amazing that no problems with homesickness have so far been encountered.

Linda is very clever, she sat down at the piano the other day and played Mozart and Beethoven and then accompanied herself, she has a lovely voice.

We have ourselves a problem: Bridget got hold of – I don't now how – a fairly large supply of Dextropor. It is to give us extra energy and it tastes very good. A substitute for sweets. We told ourselves that we needed something to keep up our strength, as we are on the go from morning to night. But now we have put on a lot of weight!

Just at the end of our road thirty boys are housed, they have one teacher and one Hitler Youth leader to look after them. We have met Martin, he is one of the best, very capable, mature and sincere, and like us in his last year at school.

Christmas is approaching and the children will be away

from home for most of them for the first time - and for us too.

21st December, 1940

Winter solstice! We celebrated it as we have done for a few years. Martin and his boys prepared a bonfire somewhere in a sheltered place amongst the dunes.

After dark, in the early evening, we marched the girls over the dunes and along the beach. It was not a bad night, light enough to find our way. We stood in a semi-circle around the fire, looking out over the sea and into the glow of the fire and celebrated the return of the light and the sun. I am sure I was not alone in thinking of brighter days when there was no war and no danger to our loved ones. We are so sheltered here, so removed from the events of the war and so busy with our task at hand, it is quite a different world.

22nd December, 1940

We keep the children busy and try to create a Christmas atmosphere. We even make our own candles and we are keeping a look-out for places where we can gather greenery – there are no Christmas trees around.

For the Christmas Day entertainment Linda is organising a performance of a fairy tale 'King Drosselbart'. Linda is marvellous, she wrote the dialogue, organised the rehearsals and costumes and plays the leading part. Everybody works with enthusiasm. Linda wants me to speak the prologue.

23rd December, 1940

I had a Christmas card from Rudi. He says he is writing on behalf of his family but we never had a card from them before, so it must be from him to me. I am so happy! I would like to sit down and reply immediately but I must not – not yet – I don't want to give away my feelings. I decided to wait four weeks, but no longer!

24ᵗʰ December, 1940

It is late. We got through Christmas Eve without upsets. In the afternoon we took the girls for a long walk and when they returned the dining hall looked very festive. The tables were laid for a special supper and there were parcels to be unpacked. No time to think of home and cry.

26ᵗʰ December, 1940

Our play was a great success. Christmas passed without any problems.

Early January, 1941

Mum is coming to visit me here for my birthday. Nobody else has had a visitor yet but I have cleared it with Eve. It will be lovely for Mum to see the beauty of this island.

21ˢᵗ January, 1941

Mum has been here for a few days. It is a bit difficult. I must continue with my duties. But tonight we will have a little get-together in celebration of my 18ᵗʰ birthday. I have written to Rudi!

23ʳᵈ January, 1941

I have been told that it is wrong that my mother should be here and worse that she should sleep in the little room (where I make up a bed for her every night) adjacent to the dining hall. I pleaded that it was only for another two nights. I feel very bad, both for my mother and also because I don't want to claim any privileges.

25ᵗʰ January, 1941

I was allowed a day off and I took Mum back as far as Danzig. What a beautiful town it is and German through and through. It dates back to 1300 but acquired real importance when in 1361 it joined the Hanseatic

Confederation of North German Harbour Towns, that exercised great power thanks to their world-wide trade. We saw the famous and picturesque Krantor, the gothic cathedral and walked along the streets famous for their patrician houses. They have narrow fronts (local taxes were charged according to the width of the house) but are very spacious thanks to their depth. At the end of the first World War Danzig was declared a Free City under the League of Nations' protection.

Another emotional farewell from Mum.

February, 1941

Yesterday I walked along the beach and noticed on the horizon a slim, silver lining. When I returned this morning there was ice as far as I could see. Large floats of ice pushing into each other – a mighty, beautiful sight. The silver lining I saw was the ice being swept towards the land.

We had a visitor, one of the higher-ups of the local Hitler Youth. We didn't like him at all. When we gathered in the evening in Martin's place he suggested parlour games that led to kissing – we were pretty disgusted.

We are going to repeat our 'King Drosselbart' in Hela and Neustadt for the local people – quite an honour.

Martin is having a problem with one of his boys. He is a very strong boy, very mature for his fourteen years. He would walk through fire for Martin, but he seems to be attracted to one of our girls. The sort of girl that would start early in life making eyes at the boys. It seems a very strong attraction and we have to watch them carefully. Martin will have a serious talk with the boy.

We have our own, unusual problems. One of the girls complained of abdominal pains and was running a temperature. We have no medical help here. We never expected any serious illness. Bridget, who has an interest in medicine, feared appendicitis and we had to organise a car to take the girl to hospital in Neustadt – an hour's drive away.

10 Days Later

Since then we had another three girls going down with the same symptoms, one after the other. We put them in the sick-room and took it in turns keeping watch at their bedside right through the night. They became delirious and we were really worried. In the end an ambulance came from Zoppot, but it took hours to arrive. Nobody ever heard of an appendicitis epidemic. But they couldn't just have put it on?

Another letter from Rudi. He too, escaped the final examination at school. He has to do his Labour Service. He would rather have joined the army. These boys are so impatient to do their bit and are afraid the war might be over before they had their chance.

March, 1941

Martin had a wonderful idea, he is taking his boys to the casino building and down to the subterranean rooms - we discovered a network of passages and rooms, all very dark – to tell them ghost stories by the light of a few candles. But we are to follow them and make ghostly noises that will echo around the passages.

Three Days Later

Our ghost session was a great success but the boys were not taken in for long and started chasing us.

Now that the days are longer we can keep the girls outdoors a little more. There is a disused ship on the Haff and Linda, who can be quite a tomboy, has devised a wonderful game. She will defend the ship with her crew, whilst the rest of us will be the pirates out to overpower them.

Late March, 1941

We have been so engrossed in our life on the peninsula and our duties in keeping the children happy, that the rest of the world has receded. The girls too, must be feeling that way because we have to remind them to write home after some anxious parents had contacted us, having heard nothing from their daughters.

But now the other world is catching up with us. Martin has been called up into the army; our school year is coming to an end and Linda and Barbara are talking of returning home and the political events are making headlines again. We have come to agreements with Hungary, Rumania and Bulgaria but Greece has stood up to the Italian invasion. The Italians are not much help to us! There has also been talk all the time of our invasion of England.

1ˢᵗ April, 1941
I have volunteered to stay on for another six months.

7ᵗʰ April, 1941
Now there is a real war again. We have marched into Yugoslavia and Greece. I am sure we have no designs on these countries but Rommel and his army are already fighting in Libya. Could it be that the enemy could reach us, through the back-door, as it were?

I have received my school certificate, at least it arrived at home. As expected, only in Literature and History did I get good marks, all the rest is shades of 'passed'; at least I did not fail.

May, 1941
I said a sad farewell to Jurata. It has been a wonderful time; my friends have already gone but we have promised that we shall keep in touch. These six months will be a strong bond. I am having a short holiday and then I have been told to take up a secondment with a school evacuated to a place near Graudenz. I am not looking forward to it.

7ᵗʰ May, 1941
It is good to be home again. How one gets lost in ones own world. Air-raids had lost all their horror.

11th May, 1941

It is not possible, Rudolf Hess has flown to England. The radio announced it and said he had lost his reason, he was mad.

13th May, 1941

We met my aunt Lisa today. It was to be an outing to the Muggelsee. We used to go there once or twice a year, the woods are lovely and I was looking forward to meeting my aunt. She has her elderly mother to look after – the mother refuses to go into the air-raid shelter but stays in her flat and does not even turn the lights off. This is very dangerous in the centre of Berlin. But as we were walking I could not stop thinking about Rudolf Hess. He was never much in the limelight, not like Góring who loves showing off his medals or Goebbels who is not really loved by anyone. Now they say Hess is a traitor who went over to the enemy. I had a violent argument with my mother and aunt. Whatever Hess did, he could never be a traitor!

(ii)   Zoppot

Early July, 1941

No entry for two months!

I was sent to this small school, only about 25 girls, but it was all so different. The school teacher was in charge and had it all organised down to one afternoon a week when all the girls sat down to write home. I didn't like it, but I could not have made any changes, not after six months. So I was glad to move on again.

On 22nd June, a new phase in the war began. We are now fighting in the East, our troops marched into the Soviet Union. There seems to be next to no resistance. It strikes me as strange that after we signed a peace pact with Stalin, we are now at war. But then the Führer has always said that Germany needs to expand to the East. Right through history we have gone East to conquer and cultivate.

I am in Zoppot, once a fashionable seaside place. Our home is quite near to the sea and again the two school teachers seem to run the show. The girls are not very keen on listening to lectures, all they want is to go swimming. I have watched them from the pier, diving into the water from quite a few metres above the water level and I hate jumping and I cannot dive properly.

Two Weeks Later

I have been here a couple of weeks now. Every morning when the girls are having their lessons I go down to the sea and try diving but so far I always land on my tummy and my thighs are blue with bruises.

End July, 1941

The girls are on holiday now and I made it!! I suddenly got the knack of the diving. I went into the water arms and head first and the legs following. No big splash, it really feels good!

One of the teachers here has an interest in opera and she took me to the open-air theatre here in Zoppot where an opera season is in progress. We saw 'The Mastersingers'. It was wonderful – once again and so unexpected. The only strange thing was that for the night scene, when all the burghers of Nuremberg rush out into the street (in their night clothes) and a fight develops, it was still daylight. But in the last act, when all the Guilds assemble on the common for a great festival, night had fallen and artificial light had to reproduce a sunlit day of celebrations.

I have been promised another visit to hear 'Tannhäuser'.

August, 1941
I had to go into the harbour area on some business. I had not realised it was such a large and confusing complex, so I had to ask my way. The man I approached seemed to work in the harbour. He took me to my destination and offered to wait to return me to the exit. It was a long walk and we talked a lot. Unfortunately, as it turned out, I told him why I was in Zoppot and gave away my address. I couldn't have guessed what was to follow. Before we reached the exit he proposed marriage! I was so taken aback, I didn't know what to say. He seemed a very lonely person and I did not want to hurt his feelings. Of course, I should have just laughed and walked away.

Two Days Later
He has been asking for me! I warned everybody now not to let him in and to say that I was not available.

I wrote to Mum telling her my story.

Later in August
We went to hear 'Tannhäuser'. It was even more impressive. I love the music. What it must feel like to conduct this glorious pilgrims' march! The scene was unforgettable.

The theatre was built in a small valley and a wooded hill rises gently behind the stage. Through the woods the pilgrims approached from quite a distance, winding their way through the trees on their return from Rome; the sound of the voices swelling as they draw nearer and all this under the star-lit sky. What a memory to take away!

As the last chords of the opera died away my companion said she knew the tenor and we would go to the artists' room to find him. We did – he came to the door but disclaimed all knowledge of the lady!

A reply from Mum came – what a disappointment. She quite misunderstood me. She said that if I liked the man I should see him! That was not at all what I wanted. How difficult it is to explain something by letter!

September, 1941

Our troops are marching so fast into Russia – they are no match for our soldiers. But there was a very heavy air-raid on Berlin. Despite these raids there is talk that our schools may all return to Berlin. Perhaps the parents think that one year without their children is enough. Perhaps the teachers have been agitating. It is worse in Berlin now than it was a year ago; but maybe people got used to it.

I heard from Rudi. He is in the army now and under training; he cannot wait to join the action.

Late September, 1941

Yes, the girls are all returning home within a few days. I shall be staying on for two or three days and then it will be home for me too.

LABOUR SERVICE

October, 1941

Home again. The war is moving further away from us in the East.

But what am I to do with myself now?

Yesterday, we were just having lunch when aunt Martha called with a message from Rudi. He was given a few hours to see his family to say 'good-bye'. He borrowed a bike to cycle over to his village and asked if we could be at the railway station at 4.00 p.m. to see him off. Of course we could! Mum, Jurgen and I went and he came with his aunt and uncle and also his sister. He looked so tall and smart in his uniform. He is off to North Africa – to Rommel's desert fight - and very excited.

When the train drew in we shook hands but when he bent down to kiss his sister he looked at me and smiled. I will always remember that smile. We were very sad walking home. It is the first time someone really close went to face the dangers of the war.

My immediate problem is solved. This morning I received my orders to serve six months in the 'Arbeitsdienst', at a place Borken in what used to be the Polish Corridor. I have only a week to get ready – poor Mum.

I had not really expected to have to serve these six months, not after a year of voluntary service in the evacuation. Still, the Führer introduced this idea of every young person doing six months of manual work. Many of us would never be required to do this kind of work and what is more, one meets with people from many walks of life and all that can only be good and promote understanding.

One week later

The day of yet another parting came. Mum took me to

the station in Berlin. The platform was swarming with girls, each clutching a little suitcase. There was a long wait – someone started 'Lily Marlene' and the song spread down the platform until we were all singing.

Mid-October, 1941

We survived the first twenty-four hours. Borken is a very small place and a dull one too. Our new 'home' is right at the end of the main street and next to the church. We are about forty-five girls, split into three groups. Each group in a bedroom with double bunks – I secured a top one. This bed, a small wardrobe and a chair is all we have plus one communal table. The girls seem to be nice enough, most of them come from the Hanover area. There is one large room next to ours on the ground floor, where we shall gather for meetings.

We started with receiving our uniforms. A cotton dress for work, skirt, blouse and jacket for going out and more formal occasions. Our own clothes we can forget for six months. Oh yes, we also have a coat, hat, gloves and shoes, all in khaki colours.

There are four people running the camp. They have various duties and a Miss Kruger is in charge. She looks as if she is not all that happy with her job.

It appears that we shall be confined to the camp for the first two weeks, sharing in all the domestic tasks and then we shall be sent out to the farms in the neighbourhood.

A Few Days Later

Mum sent on a letter from Rudi. He is in Italy, full of enthusiasm and also full of praise for Chianti wine!

Early December, 1941

We have been out to 'our' farms. How can I describe this experience? First of all, there are no villages here as I know them from home. Most of the farms are isolated places in the midst of acres of flat, agricultural land. These farms belonged to Polish people who were disowned by us – how they must hate us – after our successful war in 1939. The farms were then given to German settlers, repatriated from Russia under the terms of our Friendship Treaty with Stalin. It seems these families came back willingly even though they had lived in Russia for generations. It is extraordinary, they still speak German with the dialect of the area from which their ancestors originated.

But how they live now! I don't know whether words can describe it! The house has no heating except for the cooker in the kitchen, no water – there is a well outside into which buckets are lowered to fetch up the water. The only furniture in the kitchen is a large table, some chairs and a doorless cupboard. In that room live the husband and wife, four children, a somewhat mentally retarded relative and a Polish farmworker, plus a cat and half a dozen chickens; they, the chickens, have the free run of the room and are often seen inside the cupboard. There is a small room next to the kitchen where I have spent my first two days of secondment. I was asked if I could sew and was handed a large basket of mending. It will take days to work through that and I noticed a sewing machine in the corner.

The farmer's wife looks as if she is nearing fifty, but the children are quite young. The smallest is only a baby, so she must be quite a young person.

From 'my' room I can look into the bedrooms – two of them – with five beds in all, so they must be sleeping two to a bed. The rooms are all so bare, no carpets, no ornaments.

*　　　*　　　*

Our day starts at 6.00 a.m. when a loud voice calls us from our slumber. We are expected to jump from our bunks – not exactly jump when one is in the upper one! We then dive into our tracksuits and line up outside for early morning exercises and a quick jog around the church yard, which, in the dark, is more stumbling than jogging. Then we wash and dress and again assemble outside to hoist the flag with a short ceremony of reading and singing. After breakfast we are off at 8.00 a.m. For me, and some others, it is an hour's walk along country lanes to my farm.

Of course, the idea is that we help with the farm work, but there is hardly any now. We stay until 3.00 p.m. and then march 'home' again. During the afternoon we have lectures and other organised activities. Perhaps some free time on Sunday?

We do hear the latest news from the front, our troops are still moving East. The Führer's strategy is to move forward in two arms, overtake the enemy, close the circle behind him and then there is no escape. It works wonderfully well.

Late November, 1941

I begged my farmer that he should let me do some outdoor work, so they let me take the horse round and round in the yard threshing corn – I don't think it was much of a help to them.

Early December, 1941

No letter from Rudi – perhaps they take longer from Africa.

I am doing more and more sewing for my family, especially since they found out that I can use the sewing machine. The little girl keeps me company sometimes. Despite the squalor I like the family very much. I tried to make a pair of shoes for the girl, she has none and is in trouble with the school for not attending.

These people are almost unworldly, when they buy their monthly rations, they eat well and then they go without for a couple of weeks. I suppose they have never been short of food before. A few days ago the wife baked bread, she must have done it late at night by the light of a petrol lamp and the bread, which is usually mouth-watering, tasted of petrol.

Our troops are within sight of Moscow, but winter is setting in.

8th December, 1941

We heard that Japan has attacked Pearl Harbour, many ships went down. It must have been a complete surprise and now America has joined the war – it is ominous!

I heard from Eileen that I have been accepted as a member of the NSDAP. Not everybody can join these days, but some of those active as leaders in the Hitler Youth are chosen when they reach the age of 18.

Mid-December, 1941

We have been told that we shall be allowed to go home for Christmas, only two or three will have to stay behind.

20th December, 1941

The news from the Russian front is not good. This was the last day with my family, when we come back after Christmas we shall all be changed around to other families. I am very sorry; they gave me such a send-off. I must have been talking, saying that food is not plentiful at home. I came away with a parcel of meat, a large salami sausage, bacon and a piece of pork. (They had killed a pig recently.) I am looking forward to seeing Mum's face! It was so kind of these people!

21st December, 1941

Our last day. Later today we are going to bring a little Christmas spirit to our families. We shall be going in small groups to their homes and sing Christmas carols and some of our new, very beautiful songs and light a few candles.

I am developing a nasty, large, septic place on my hand.

23rd December, 1941

I am home again in my own room. Mum was overjoyed

to see me back. Aunt Anna is already here for Christmas. When I unpacked my food parcel Mum's eyes almost popped out. She says she will share some of it with her sister and her brother and their families. She will see them tomorrow. I also brought a small Christmas tree but Mum managed to get one even though they are in very short supply, so she will take one to her sister.

The journey home was very bad. My hand was throbbing so badly I hardly slept the last night in the camp. Our I.C. Medicals said she was not allowed to do anything so I stuck it until we reached Graudenz. When I assured myself that there was sufficient time before the departure of our next train, I just walked down the road until I found a doctor and rang the bell. He was a friendly, elderly man and he called me in and cut the boil open – what a relief! My hand was bandaged but I managed, just, to carry my luggage and the tree! The train was packed and we spent the night sitting on our bags in the corridor.

I was pretty tired when we reached Berlin. I had intended to go to the hairdressing department in Wertheim to have my hair cut and permed. I had enough of this bun at the back of my neck, so I went despite being so tired.

Tomorrow I will give Mum another surprise, she doesn't know yet that I am staying over the New Year.

1st *January, 1942*

1st January, 1942

Another year and we are still at war. It is no longer a pleasure to see a new year in. Jurgen will be 18 this year, when is he going to be called up? He lacks the enthusiasm others show. He was never very keen on the Hitler Youth either.

Sunday, 4th January, 1942

We all reported back on duty again!

I never thought the year would start like this. On Friday, I was ready to leave within a few hours; I stood at the kitchen window looking out into our little street, when I saw Aunt Martha, Rudi's aunt approaching. She smiled but my heart sank, she never visits us uninvited. The family had heard that Rudi was officially reported missing. Presumably shot down over the Mediterranean. Rudi missing, even before he reached the fighting front! We kept talking, each of us clinging to the hope that missing was not dead.

So I went off to catch my train! There was another long delay and it was cold, so I went to the cinema. The news-reel was full of pictures from Africa and Rommel's successes. I could hardly bare to look.

I didn't tell anybody here but in bed I could not stop crying. The morning is almost worse, one wakes and for a second there is still calm within and then the knowledge of what happened floods back.

7th January, 1942

There is only one large house in the village, the Squire's place and I have been sent there for the sole purpose of looking after one small child – I hate it!

10th January, 1942

I have been relieved of that job, I shall be going to another farm.

Late January, 1942

I have been asked to plan some entertainment for the rest of the camp. That is, each room will think of something to surprise the others. As I am Speaker for our room it will have to be me to come up with an idea – which I already have - I shall emulate the radio Request Concert! As there are only fifteen of us in the room it will be a bit of a squeeze. We need a military band, a chorus and a lot of soloists. I have already talked one of the girls to taking over as Compère, Heinz Goedicke, but my first task is to write, in verse, the commentary. From now on, as we walk to our farms and on the way home, I compose my bits of poetry and scribble them down – not at all easy when it is dark and very, very cold and when we stumble through the snow across the fields.

February, 1942

I learnt a lesson worth remembering!

Some of the girls have for some time been complaining that their letters have been opened and read. Somehow, during yesterday afternoon's lecture, there was an opportunity to air that grievance and I spoke up. Our Miss Kruger gave me a very nasty look and asked for specific cases. I looked around for the girls who had spoken to me, but all remained silent. So I had to withdraw and apologise! Never again will I speak for others!

Mid-February, 1942

Our 'concert' is almost ready. We have a tenor, Sara Leander, three Hawaiian dancers (skirts of straw over sport's trunks) a.s.o. I am just amazed how willingly the girls give up their free afternoons to rehearse and prepare. I get on better with them than the younger girls I used to lead. Minchen is spending her free time behind the office typewriter typing the script for our show.

A Few Days Later

We gave our 'concert'. A few things went wrong which only added to the fun, it was a great success. Somehow I think I surprised everybody. They thought I would do something really Germanic! Now it is the turn of the others to entertain us in a few weeks' time.

End of February, 1942

There are so many air-raids on German towns now, it is worrying, but here we are so far from it all.

We had our last change-over of duties. I am on the indoors team. Two weeks' cleaning, two weeks' laundry and two weeks' kitchen.

April, 1942

Our last day – we have handed back our uniforms – how different it is to see everybody in civilian clothes; uniforms are such levellers, differences in background and education fade into insignificance. I will keep in touch with Irmela, she lives not very far from us.

SECRETARIAL COLLEGE

April, 1942

Home once more! I have been thinking and talking to Mum. I am nineteen now, most of my friends are in jobs, earning money and I haven't even started to learn something useful. So there is no choice but to go for an office job – I shall enrol for a 6-months course at the Rackow School. The very thing I did not want to do; serves me right for looking down on girls who selected a secretarial career.

A Little Later in April

I now have a season ticket for my daily trip to Berlin and the College. I am back at school, but I am also, once again, Gruppenführerin in Mahlow.

May, 1942

We are making pretty fast progress particularly in typing and shorthand, there isn't that much time, only six months. Book-keeping is quite good. We also have some sort of history lessons but there are three students in the class – two boys and a girl (they are the best in our group) – who are very anti-Hitler and they have a very clever way of making their disapproval known – it annoys and worries me.

June, 1942

The situation in the East has been worrying since our advances came to such an abrupt end in December. We all expected the war to be over in no time. There seemed to be no resistance, but the winter must have been awful for our soldiers; out there in that vast country, in ice and snow. But we are on the move again. We must capture the rich oil fields and the industrial area.

Jurgen has been called up into the Labour Service. He too, has not finished school. I am glad I am home now, Mum would be on her own with Grandad.

I had a terrible experience yesterday. I was on the train to Berlin – I had to return to school for some afternoon engagement. Between Mahlow and Lichtenrade the train travels through agricultural land and passes a little-used level crossing. At that point we came to a sudden halt. After a while we realised that there had been an accident. We all left the train and, having had some first-aid training, I felt obliged to have a closer look. The train had collided with a farm tractor. A Polish farm worker had been thrown twenty-five metres and lay dead on the embankment, the farmer was no longer a human body and there was a little blond boy, apparently the grandson, still breathing but with a terrible head wound. What was there to do? It took a dreadfully long time before a doctor arrived. I went home feeling sick, unable to think of anything but that unfortunate family.

*   *   *

At school we are also studying French and English business correspondence. We have to compose short letters, placing orders or acknowledging correspondence, but I don't seem able to get anything right. I think the teacher has given me up. I am, naturally, not very fond of her.

*   *   *

Our troops have reached Stalingrad. General Paulus's 6th Army is encircling the town. It is a very important place, both for the Russians and us.

July, 1942
Our garden is lovely now, even though Mum has

enlarged the vegetable plot. As children we used to play table tennis on the dining table, much endangering all the large vases and ornaments that stood on the shelf above the old-fashioned high-back sofa. Now we play sometimes in the garden. Mum produced a croquet set for us. We play it on the lawn. I think it reminds Mum of her young days when they played it on her grand-father's big lawn. It was a game young ladies in long skirts could play.

Every day when I walk home and look across the gardens to our house I think perhaps, just perhaps, there could be a letter from Rudi, he could have survived – but there never is one.

August, 1942

My uncle Werner found a job in Frankfurt after his return from Brazil. His family lives there now but he was posted to Russia. There are so many engineering projects, rebuilding what was destroyed during the fighting, to secure the supply for our troops. Mum has arranged with my aunt that I am to spend a week in Frankfurt.

Frankfurt, August, 1942

Frankfurt seems a very attractive city. We live near a beautiful park. My aunt goes out to work but my cousin is on school holidays. Our age difference does not show so much now – we shall be having fun together.

*　　　　*　　　　*

My aunt allowed us to have a day out in the Taunus. We took a tram into the hilly, lovely woods. We found lots of raspberries and blueberries but were not prepared for such a find. On the way home the juice started dripping from our make-shift containers, which we had placed on the rack above our heads. We thought it was very funny, only the other travellers did not agree!

September, 1942

Mum has given me a wonderful surprise. She went to the Reichskanzlei at the Wilhelmplatz and boldly asked if there were vacancies for secretaries and whether anybody could apply. She was told 'yes'; one should write to 'The Kanzlei des Führers'. Mum cannot have found that easy and I am not sure she wants me to work in such a place but she must have sensed how unhappy I am in training to be a secretary and taking a job in any odd office. I shall write my application straight away.

We are really working hard for our examinations at the end of our course. Strangely, I have never taken an examination, except one after a first-aid course with the Red Cross.

*   *   *

Our troops reached the outskirts of Stalingrad, but the fighting is heavy and progress slow – we had expected a quick success, but the Russians are showing unusual resistance.

The Führer spoke, he said we would take Stalingrad – he has never let us down.

October, 1942

I have been offered an interview! Hurray! Hurray!

Jurgen has been called up into the Army. He is only eighteen. Mum is very brave about it; but with the heavy fighting at Stalingrad and the winter approaching … …

All around us the boys are disappearing into the army. Gunther, opposite us, is an only child, the parents are not so young, the mother an invalid, the grand-parents do all the work in the garden and house.

Mid-October, 1942

What a day! I went for my interview. I was told to use

the entrance in the Voss Strasse, just behind the store Wertheim. I walked up the very broad stairs to the top where two S.S. men in their black uniforms guard the door. I was permitted to enter – the door is enormously large, leading into a very spacious hall. At a desk I produced my letter and was taken by lift into the Personnel Manager's office. He was not a uniformed man and very friendly. I had to tell him all I had done in my life so far. Then he explained to me that all secretarial staff had to start in the Postal Office. The task there is to sort and index the vast amount of mail that arrives every day for the Führer. Later on I would have a chance of promotion. Then a difficulty arose. I was asked for names of referees: someone in a high position, or an old party member. But I could not think of any such person, there is nobody amongst our friends in such a position. He seemed slightly concerned but then offered me the job at DM 100 a month and said I would receive a written confirmation. I think he looked at me kindly because he had already told me that he had worked in a bank, like my father.

Now I have a job. What a job. I cannot believe it!

Our soldiers are still fighting in Stalingrad, we must achieve control of the Volga and interrupt the Russian supply route. But now the winter is near – I feel very glum when I think of our soldiers.

25th October, 1942

Mum and I have been to Küstrin to visit Jurgen before he is off to the front. We understand he will be sent to the West rather than the East, which would be a great relief to Mum. We all dread Russia and the Russians. There was no enthusiasm today – Mum is very brave.

KANZLEI DES FÜHRERS

(i)   Berlin

1ˢᵗ November, 1942

I started my job! It is such a special feeling, walking up that flight of stairs and passing the two S.S. men into the building which I shall now be allowed to enter every day. The building in which the Führer is living and working. Of course, he is now at his headquarters. I was taken up by lift, our office is right at the top of the building looking down on the Voss Strasse. I was introduced to the other staff. There are two girls, a little younger than myself, one married woman rather heavily made-up, one woman in her forties and the man in charge of us. He sits in the small room next to ours and his main task seems to be to read the mail that arrives twice a day – a whole sack full – and mark the letters up for the various departments. All these letters come from ordinary people and are addressed to the Führer. The mail then comes to us. Our room is quite large and all around the walls are boxes full of index cards. We check whether the writer has previously written to the Führer and if so the older woman, who is in charge of the archives, attaches the previous correspondence and then the lot goes to five different departments. People ask the Führer for help in legal or social difficulties, some just write with good wishes. I suppose the Führer sees none of these letters but the staff in the Kanzlei act on his behalf.

I now have a pass and can enter the building unhindered.

Early November, 1942

The news from Stalingrad is getting worse. There is still hope – there must be – as the Russians are having supply problems now the Volga is blocked by ice. We are not making progress though, every house is fought for.

The Führer let it be known that we have achieved our main objective in Stalingrad and that we will not sacrifice more troops but that the fight continues mostly from the air.

There is also a heavy battle fought in North Africa. Rommel is such a wonderful soldier and leader. Everybody thinks so highly of him. I believe ordinary people have an instinctive feeling about their leaders. Göring is popular but we make jokes about him. Goebbels is respected because he is very clever and I am sure is devoted to the Führer but nobody loves him. Himmler is not at all liked and many of the other big names seem to be rather insignificant people.

I learnt that the Head of the Kanzlei is a Mr. Bouhler and Albert Borman, the brother of Martin, also has an important position.

November, 1942
News about Stalingrad is ever more worrying. The Russians seem to have gained the upper hand, their supplies are coming in and ours have to be brought over a thousand kilometres.

Late November, 1942
The Russians have copied the Führer's strategy and they are encircling our already heavily depleted army. It is horrible to think of our brave soldiers, left there in Stalingrad, in the Russian winter, without food and no hope of getting out – or are we able to relieve them? This is the first real disaster of the war for us.

December, 1942
My job is all right. It is still a thrilling feeling to walk into the Kanzlei every day. But I don't feel quite at ease with my colleagues. They are not the type of people I expected to find here. As far as I can find out they all got their job because they had connections. I feel very proud, being the only one who secured the job on merit.

I had an idea. The girls talked about the lack of Christmas decorations, there are no trees or branches to be had in Berlin so when we make our Advent wreath at home we shall make two.

7th December, 1942

I took an earlier train today, sneaked into the office, placed the Advent wreath on the centre table, lit the candles and disappeared into the toilet only to emerge after everybody else had arrived. They were so delighted and the conversation of the morning was who might have brought the wreath? I didn't let on and they will never find out! But it made me very happy.

Is that a lesson to be remembered? My own feelings of not belonging were reflected by the other girls and then taken by me as proof that I was disliked.

The news from Stalingrad is deeply depressing. Only the badly wounded are air-lifted out - what must it feel like to be left behind in these hopeless conditions?

Our food rations are getting smaller but I get a meal in our canteen which is not bad. Jurgen is still in France but even then we don't want to think of Christmas.

31st December, 1942

Farewell to another year! There is only one wish in our hearts: that 1943 may bring peace, that the Führer may inspire us all to work and fight harder. Our soldiers have performed such great deeds, there can only by victory.

January, 1943

Our soldiers are still fighting in Stalingrad, every square metre is fought for. It must be possible to bring in some relief. General Paulus has refused to surrender.

February, 1943

The battle of Stalingrad is over! The headquarters fell

into Russian hands, surrender came on the 2nd. Shall we ever forget Stalingrad?

18th February, 1943

We have been asked to donate warm clothing, boots and skiing outfits so that they can be sent to our soldiers. Mum was not so happy when I insisted that we hand over our skis. Jurgen is not here to decide and who thinks of skiing at times like this? Of course, I understand Mum must have found it hard to scrape together the money for our outfits, but what does this count for now?

20th April, 1943

The Führer's birthday. Our mail bag was very large, so many people want to send him their good wishes. The Führer never visits Berlin now. Of course, he has to be near his soldiers, but it would be wonderful to be under the same roof with him.

A Few Days Later

I have been asked to help out in another department for a couple of days. There is a whole, huge room full of parcels, all gifts for the Führer on his birthday and they will have to be unpacked and the goods sorted.

Two Days Later

I had a wonderful time. We worked all day and through the night. What love is being showered on the Führer! All items of clothing and food will go to refugee and children camps. I walked through parts of the building I had never seen before. Through an open door I caught a glimpse of the Führer's study, a vast room, his enormous desk at the far end. Through the window I could see the trees from the garden beyond. In the evening we had a meal and a rest in a small, intimate room, just a table and benches on either side. Someone said the Führer likes meeting his old friends or comrades here. Albert Borman came in the evening to see how the work was progressing. There was so much I had to tell Mum when I arrived home.

May, 1943

We had a directive from our leadership that whenever we heard of someone whose husband or son had been killed, we should visit that family, taking flowers, to show support and sympathy. I think this is an awful idea and I could not bring myself to pay such a visit. What could I, a stranger, do to ease the grief of such families? And what if they resented me or the system that brought this war about? I feel bad disobeying an order just as I felt bad when a few years ago, membership of the Hitler Youth was made compulsory and we were asked to report to the police, girls who repeatedly missed the weekly meetings. What good would it have done to force parents to send their children? Fortunately, I never heard of anyone being reported. Most of the young girls loved coming.

Mid-July, 1943

Enemy troops have landed in Sicily. The Italians are really not much help to us in this war. If they don't resist further advances, our soldiers will have to fight on that front as well.

End-July, 1943

The news from Italy is really dreadful. The King has assumed power – he has been only a figurehead under the Duce. The Duce has been arrested and taken to the Abruzzi mountains.

Now there have been some terrible air-raids on Hamburg, not just one, but day after day and for the first time phosphorus bombs have been used. They set the town alight. One hears terrible stories of burning people rushing into the streets only to find the street alight. It is horrible and frightening.

2ⁿᵈ August, 1943 (From my diary)

Now the war seems to start in earnest for us. Cologne, Aachen, Hamburg are almost razed to the ground. Berlin is in a state of feverish excitement. Lots of people are moving out of the towns. The wildest stories are passing from mouth to mouth. If only those phosphorus bombs were not so frightening, like living torches people jumped into the water. Only four nights and a whole town in ruins!

The rumours say the Führer received an ultimatum from England. He abdicates or Berlin will be razed to the ground. How dare they! The Führer abdicating!

We moved our thousands of index cards into the basement rooms of the Kanzlei. Very good exercise! It is hard work, we crawl over boxes but our work still continues. Albert Borman came to inspect our new arrangements. It is unbelievably hot, 42°C day after day.

When the Duce abdicated on the 26th, Marshall Badoglio took over – what a disappointment that must have been for the Führer. If only there were not so many pessimists around! Our brave soldiers at the front will stand firm. All through this cruel winter they stood their ground, even though Stalingrad and the Caucasus are lost. The battle that is raging now is all defensive. Jurgen is near Charkow, he was transferred from France.

15th August, 1943

There is talk about us – our part of the Kanzlei – being evacuated.

Birthplace – with Mum and neighbours

Father with baby daughter 4 months old

First school day

1934 – with brother

On holiday – Obersee Bavaria

Rudi's Confirmation

1935 – In uniform

1939 – Our house under construction. Grandfather with workforce

1939 – Our house

1941 - Arbeitsmaid

1944 – During Anti-Aircraft Service

1944 – Mum bringing home potatoes

(ii)   Evacuation

26th August, 1943

We have left Berlin, without much notice. Our transport was by lorry and we are now in Bad Schonfliess, not far from Koenigsberg. Nothing much seems to happen here. We are in private accommodation, Irma and I share a couple of rooms, a bedroom and a sitting room. I am not sure whether the landlord couple like us very much.

9th September, 1943 (from my diary)

We have been here for three weeks, the office is fairly well established, work continues.

The latest news is that Italy capitulated. The truce was signed on 3rd September. A national government has been formed. The troops will either continue to fight with us or our soldiers will disarm them. Now our boys will have to defend this front as well. It won't be easy.

The Allies landed in Italy on 3rd September. No air-raids on Berlin this week.

23rd September, 1943 (from my diary)

The Duce has been freed! What a wonderful deed! One of our officers, Otto Skorzeny, landed with the aid of gliders and a small aircraft on the mountain and carted the Duce off to the Führer's headquarters. We were playing cards when the special news item was broadcast. What joy! At last another daring, up-lifting deed! It has done us a world of good.

We used to play table tennis every night. I enjoyed that, took me back to the days when Jurgen and Rudi played it in the lounge. One of our S.S. men is a very good player but I rarely get a chance playing against him. But now we have run out of tennis balls and have taken to playing cards. It started as a simple game and progressed to playing for money. I won DM 5 the other night. On such evenings we don't return to our quarters until 11.00 p.m. I wonder what the Superintendent, our landlord, thinks of it. But never mind him.

Had a nice letter from Val. I shall see her on Sunday.

There is still doubt as to whether we shall stay here, the talk is of somewhere nearer Berlin. It would help with the travelling but the work! We may even move into a castle. Borman was here two weeks ago and he will report to the Führer. Borman recognised me from the time when I assisted with the birthday presents.

October, 1943

My uncle Henry was killed on the Russian front. He did not want to be a soldier and had avoided quite successfully for some time to be called up. I think my grandfather took it badly.

Late October, 1943

We did something I am really ashamed of. Some of the country lanes around here are lined with apple trees and the apples are ripe now. Someone conceived the idea that we could take one of our lorries and come back with a good harvest of apples. The lorry had a canvas covering and onto it we piled the apples. What we had not anticipated was that on our return anyone watching from an upstairs window could see what we had done. Our behaviour should be beyond reproach.

12th November, 1943 (from my diary)

Everybody is ill. Irma was taken to hospital. Only two of us are left in a freezing room to get on with the work. At last someone came from Berlin and realised how cold it is – blankets arrived and new heaters.

Jurgen is on five weeks leave. I go home every Sunday. It is an awful lot of travelling. I return home during the night and arrive at 7.00 a.m. It is very tiring but otherwise very good.

27th November, 1943 (from my diary)

Now it is Berlin's turn. All the air-raids so far were child's play. Heavy attacks on the North on Thursday; Monday and Tuesday the centre: Alexander Platz, Potsdamer Platz, several Ministries in the Leipziger Strasse, all in ruins. Some of the railway stations were badly hit. No transport, people walk for hours through rubble, the smoke burns the eyes. And we sit here in safety! Yesterday another heavy attack on the North and centre. Poor Berliners – what may have happened at home?

December, 1943

I wish I had some decent clothes. All the other girls are much better dressed. Mum used to make all my dresses and it did not matter at school. Mum made up a winter coat for me, the coupons just don't allow me to buy a new one.

The air-raids go on and on, but so does life. Sometimes we catch sight of the bombers when they are visible in the searchlights, there are dozens and dozens of them and one knows they will unload their deadly cargo somewhere over Berlin.

There is a little comfort in the slow progress the Allies are making in Italy.

Saturday, 25th December, 1943 (from my diary)

Christmas Even in Schonfliess! We celebrated quite pleasantly, there was wine, lots of cake and popular music, but it was not Christmas.

And Mum alone at home with two old people, Grandad and aunt Anna.

22nd January, 1944 (from my diary)

It was my 21st birthday yesterday. We had important visitors, Borman and our Personnel Manager. They saw my cards and congratulated me. I took the opportunity of asking about me moving to another department. Later Borman offered me a lift in their cars as far as Koenigsberg so that I could get home on my birthday. I was glad. The air-raid sirens went when we reached Verneuchen. The train stopped at a very exposed place, it was a long stop. We could see the fires springing up in Berlin and hear the noise of the guns. I arrived home in the early hours of the morning.

I had a little party in the afternoon.

30th January, 1944
Another heavy air-raid last night. The Kanzlei was hit.

February, 1944
The Russians are making progress at Leningrad which never quite fell into our hands. Perhaps it was not that important but the siege lasted two and a half years. Now the Russians have broken through our lines.

End February, 1944
The Baltic States have been reoccupied by the Russians. What will happen to all the German people there?

4th March, 1944 (from my diary)
Our grandfather died very suddenly on 20th February. Mum was on her own when it happened, he had been bedridden for only two weeks. Now Mum has nobody. How lonely and worried she must be, but she never complains.

I was granted four days special leave and we buried my Grandad next to his beloved wife.

The day after the funeral my uncle Werner appeared. He had to desert his engineering projects in Russia and is now going to France. Our East front is moving back all the time, it does not look good. We all hope that once England has been beaten, we will recover the ground. My uncle confirmed that such is the mood at the front. Uncle Walter thinks otherwise but then he never had anything good to say about the Führer's great achievements.

This was the last entry from my diary.

(iii) Berlin Again

Spring 1944

I had my wish and I am back in Berlin again. I could not leave Mum alone in the house. The air-raids continue unabated, we suffered some damage to the house when a bomb came down nearby. The roof was damaged but miraculously – I don't know where the material for all the damaged houses is coming from – the repair work was done fairly quickly.

I am now a typist-secretary in another department. I don't think much of my boss – which is probably reciprocal – but there it is!

6th June, 1944

Mum's birthday and I bought us two tickets for the State Opera. It is very difficult to think of a present these days, there is nothing to buy or one needs coupons, which are in short supply. But the opera house was bombed last night and heavily damaged – that was the end of our treat! A lot of windows were broken in the Kanzlei, but nothing worse!

We now have to take it in turn to be on air-raid night duty at the Kanzlei.

The raids are worse now, the Americans fly the day-raids – hundred of them – and the British come at night. But life still continues.

8th June, 1944

The Allies landed in Normandy. Our strong defences should hold them back. The coastline is fortified from end to end. Jurgen is in France. I am glad I am home again so that Mum is not on her own.

9th June, 1944

Rommel was wounded in France. That is a terrible loss, he is such a wonderful General. We all love him.

There are rumours circulating that General Paulus, who was captured at Stalingrad, has gone over to the Russians and has formed a unit fighting with them. How can a German officer, who fought so bravely, betray his country?

July, 1944
I was on air-raid duty overnight. There is a tele-printer in one of the offices. If urgent messages have to go out during the night, during or after alarms, I would have to operate the printer. I hate such gadgets and a short introduction to its operation means nothing to me. I was scared! Fortunately, reams of messages came in – all about the damage done by the bombs, in minute detail – but nothing had to be sent out. What a relief!

The Russians are advancing westwards, when will it stop?

20ᵗʰ July, 1944
I had just come home when there was a news flash on the radio. An attempt has been made on the Führer's life! A bomb was placed in the room where he was holding discussions with his Generals. But the Führer is safe. He suffered only light burns and bruises. Providence has, once again, saved him for us.

21ˢᵗ July, 1944
The Führer spoke – now we really know that he is safe and sound. He said only a small group of officers were involved, their intention was to remove the Führer and at the same time kill some of those closest to him and to overthrow the High Command of the Armed Forces.

It is shameful that German officers should contemplate such an evil deed when our country is fighting a war.

28ᵗʰ July, 1944
Dr. Goebbels spoke the other day. He knows how to rally everybody behind the Führer and today he has

declared total war, everything must be directed towards the war effort. Nothing else matters. There is so little I can do! My work at the Kanzlei is not really important.

One of my colleagues has been called to the Führer's Headquarters, a new secretary is wanted. She was not chosen but what a privilege, what an enviable chance, to be interviewed by the Führer.

My cousin Harry has been called up into the army – he is only a boy.

August, 1944

The news from the front is most depressing now, our armies are moving back all the time. It is usually reported as a strategic withdrawal but we cannot go on like that, or can we?

We have had one or two film shows at the Kanzlei, we see the films before they are released to the public. I suppose to test how they are received. We saw a lovely one about three soldiers passing through Berlin on leave and meeting three pretty young girls. We know war is not like that but it is refreshing to see a light-hearted side.

All around us the boys of my age are being killed in the fighting, two from our streets. It is frightening.

Our V-bombs are hitting England. They fly across the sea unmanned, drop without warning. They must be doing great harm.

12th September, 1944

There is heavy fighting going on at Arnheim. We have successfully fought back the British troops who were trying to take the bridge and break through our Siegfried line.

20th September, 1944

I am going to have a week's holiday in Bad Reinerz. Mum has been there with her friend. She asked me if I wanted to go with them or later with Traute. I opted for the latter but felt guilty about it. I am sure Mum had hoped I would join them – was I very selfish?

22nd September, 1944

We have arrived. Our bed and breakfast place is a little primitive but Bad Reinerz is very attractive with a Kurpark and elegant streets.

The train from Berlin was crowded. I did not feel very comfortable as we are not supposed to travel for pleasure. The slogan is "wheels must roll for victory". I had a piece of paper from the Kanzlei saying that I was entitled to use the train, but when I showed it to the Inspector and he handed it back to me without a word, I felt ashamed. It was setting a bad example.

24th September, 1944

We are having quite an enjoyable time, mostly walking in the woods. We nearly got into trouble today. We had crossed the Czech frontier and hurried back – it gave us a shock.

25th September, 1944

The town is full of soldiers. Most of them convalescing. But of course, there is no entertainment in the evenings. Dancing has been prohibited for a long time.

3rd October, 1944

The Americans have broken through our defences in the West – when will it stop?

October, 1944

I have received my marching orders once again! It is all rather mysterious. I have to report to Gluckstadt in Schleswig Holstein in ten days' time. Word has gone round that the Führer wants all the fighting-fit men released from the anti-aircraft search-light units and replaced by women. Those born 1922/23 are the first to be called up.

Of course, I told my bosses and they don't want to let me go. They registered their objections with the military authorities.

There is a tug-of-war going on over me. It is not really about me but more that the Kanzlei does not wish to take orders from anybody. But I want to go now. I shall be of more use in the forces, if that is where I am wanted. So I told them that I am going. I heard that even our top secretary has volunteered for the Red Cross.

I am worried about Mum though, she will be all alone at home.

ANTI-AIRCRAFT UNITS

October, 1944

We have arrived in Gluckstadt – hundreds of us. First event was kitting-out with our uniforms. It was very funny. We filed past a Sergeant who 'measured' us with experienced eyes and threw into our outstretched arms trousers, jackets, caps, boots and a large overcoat. It appears that we shall be wearing the blue Luftwaffe uniform on duty and the khaki Arbeitsdienst clothes off-duty. At least that includes a skirt and blouse.

I don't think we shall be here for long.

Three Days Later

We were split into small groups and I am now somewhere near Hamburg in rather primitive accommodation next to 'our' anti-aircraft searchlights. The landscape around here is bleak but working with searchlights looks reasonably easy.

The difference now is that when the enemy aircraft are coming over at night – and they seem to come our way across the North Sea – we are out instead of in a shelter.

Next Day

We have already learnt that it is not at all easy to catch an aircraft in the beam of light and even more difficult to follow it and hold it.

16th October, 1944

Rommel is dead! He fell victim of an accident. What a loss! He was our most popular and successful General. His soldiers loved him, we all loved him. He is having a State funeral.

We had a real telling off today! A lot of enemy aircraft came over during the day and dropped propaganda leaflets, they rained down all around us. We rushed out to collect them, it was fun. I had never read enemy propaganda. But our Sergeant shouted at us. It was dangerous. Low-flying aircraft might have shot at us and reading enemy leaflets was treason!

A Week Later

I am now doing a specialised training under a dashing Lieutenant. We all do our best to impress him with our work. I have a rather unfair advantage over the other girls. They had only an elementary school education and when it comes to electrical diagrams and other technical theory, they are fairly lost. Physics was never my strong point, but I can stand up and explain relays and the flow of electric currents. I was rather pleased with myself but then we were taken to our search lights and had a look inside this box of tricks, one maze of wires and coils and connections – so different from the drawings on the blackboard – I shall never cope with that!

November, 1944

For the last two weeks we have been doing practical work. Every morning we are taken to a workshop. Our task is to dismantle a 4-stroke engine and then put it together again. The latter is the more problematic! There are frequent air-raid alarms. Hamburg is not a safe place.

Mid-November, 1944

Another move! I have been picked to go on a special course – probably for several months. We shall be trained as maintenance staff. When we have successfully completed our training we shall be attached to a number of units, either to carry out the repairs ourselves or to report the fault in detail to a specialist unit!

My cousin Harry was killed at the Western front near Arnhem. He died on the 24th September when I was on holiday with his sister – it does not seem fair!

EarlyDecember, 1944

We are at Greifswald, a small town at the Baltic, with the Isle of Rügen just across the water.

There are about a thousand girls here. We live in barracks with reasonable facilities. At the end of our corridor is a large shower room where I have decided to finish each day with a cold shower – just to be heroic. Our day is to be divided between practical work in the workshops and hangers in the morning and theoretical work in the classroom in the afternoon.

December, 1944

We spent the morning on the parade ground being taught the finer points of right and left turns and marching in a straight line! I can see that the military are better at that than I ever was when I marched my girls through our home streets. But will it help winning the war?

Christmas is approaching but there is no chance this time of going home. I am worried about Mum. She has nobody now and Jurgen has been posted back to the eastern front. I suppose aunt Anna will visit over Christmas.

22nd December, 1944

We had an evening off and went into town. We got talking to a group of soldiers. One of them wants to see me again but I am not in the least interested. He turned up today with a small Christmas tree. I had, unfortunately, mentioned that we could not find one.

24th December, 1944

Christmas Eve; what a wonderful day it used to be. It is not possible to ignore it so we sat together in the evening and tried to make it a bit special. Mum's parcel had arrived with a cake, which we shared. Rations are now so small that she must have been saving up for it for a long time.

January, 1945

It is very cold now and the mornings in the workshops are very uncomfortable. We wear our out-sized overcoats and very large boots.

One of the things I find hardest to bear is that one can never be alone, even for a minute (except in the loo.) I didn't feel it in Jurata, but then we formed real friendships, in Borken I had the long, lonely walks every day to the farm and in Schonfliess I could go home at weekends, but here … … I tried to sneak away for a walk but even then one of my room mates – quite a nice girl – offered to accompany me. Next time I must really keep it secret.

Later in January, 1945

We had a black-out during our afternoon lectures. We sat around a table and suddenly it was pitch-dark. When we heard the door open and close we knew our Instructor had left the room and the Viennese girl – usually a very quiet girl – started telling us Viennese jokes. They all concern two fictitious characters and very funny too. Shortly, two girls from the Rhineland, not wanting to be left out, commenced on their stories, centred on two, very different characters. A wonderful time we had! When the lights came on again, there was our Instructor sitting at the back of the room, greatly amused.

I wondered afterwards, how different humour is in different parts of our country. A true Berliner would not have seen the joke in any of these stories.

Perhaps this is one of the reasons why since 1933 deliberate attempts have been made to bring together people from all corners of our country so that we should think as Germans and not as Prussians, Saxons, a.s.o. Yet, only the other day one of the Bavarian girls told me that she thought me quite a nice person, but she quickly added that she would never marry a Prussian. I don't think we, in the North, feel that way. Though we do find the Bavarians lacking a little in military discipline and application to duty.

February, 1945

Our enemies are closing in all around us. In the West we are already defending our own borders. We are told of wonderful new weapons which are on the way – but they will have to come soon. It is just not possible that we should lose this fight. It is unthinkable that the Russian hordes should be allowed to enter our country. I often remember our families in Borken, they left Russia to return to their homeland, full of trust in finding a better life. Now they are fleeing from the Russians with the few possessions they can take with them.

There were some terrible air-raids on Dresden. Such a lovely old town and I am sure without much industry. They say there were thousands of refugees in the town. That must have been known to the British. Killing all those helpless people!

The front in the East seems to be static and our defences are holding.

March, 1945

Our food is terrible now. We don't get much at lunch-time. Nearly always a soup. As a sweet the canteen puts out a large tray of yoghurt, very watery and without sugar. In the evening we collect our daily ration of bread, butter, sausage or cheese. It makes a good meal, but it includes our breakfast ration. The trouble is we eat it all in the evening and then go without food until lunch the following day. We are, in short, very hungry.

The Allies have crossed the Rhine. So much of our industry is located there. How do we manage to carry on? Our training continues. The course should finish by the end of April.

1ˢᵗ April, 1945

Word is going around that our Commandant requested permission from the Führer Headquarters to let us all go home, but the reply was in the negative. Nothing has been said officially. The Russian forces have stopped at the Oder, some distance from here. Is the Commandant worried how to protect us from the hordes? Dreadful tales circulate as to how the women suffer.

Monday, 16th April, 1945

Yesterday morning, we were told that we are no longer wanted at Greifswald, we were being sent home. Word has it that the Commandant gave the order without reference to Headquarters. We spent the morning handing back our uniform, except our heavy overcoat, and all our study books. We collected our provisions for the last time and packed our few belongings. We are all hoping to make home but for some this is very doubtful. The Bavarian girls were quite sure that they will not make it as the south of the country is already cut off. There was much speculation and anxiety.

It was already dark when we arrived at the railway station. There were no scheduled trains but we spotted a goods train and on enquiring found that it was due to leave for Berlin. Nobody seemed to mind when we climbed aboard. Surprisingly it steamed off fairly soon and we travelled through the night without too many stops and reached the outskirts of Berlin in the early hours of the morning. I don't know what I had expected but the trains were running through Berlin and there was no difficulty in catching my train from Potsdamer Platz to Mahlow. I was home soon after breakfast time. Mum was so relieved. No news from Jurgen.

THE END

Monday, 16th April, 1945

I am home. Aunt Anna is here, Traute has come home too. She was away for the last few months, evacuated with her Ministry. She had a terrible time coming back, narrowly avoiding travelling on a train which was subsequently attacked from the air – many died.

Our mood is in strange contrast to the Spring around us. The tender green of the trees, the lilac almost ready to burst open. We listen to the news, the Führer promised us the new weapons that would turn the tide. Instead; the Russians attacked at the Oder, a fierce battle is in progress. Did I get home with just a few hours to spare?

I notice my Hitler Youth uniform has disappeared and so have my books. The Führer's "Mein Kampf", the many diaries of Dr. Goebbels, all those lovely picture books "The Führer and his Youth". Mum was somewhat vague when I asked her.

Tuesday, 17th April, 1945

There is a lot of talk now about the "Werewolf", the name given to the young boys – and possibly girls – who will fight the enemy as a last stand.

My uncle is a part-time soldier, he has been serving with the anti-aircraft units for some months but comes home between spells of duty.

We hear terrible stories from the East, women raped and maltreated by the Russians. It just cannot happen here!

Wednesday, 18th April, 1945

The air-raids continue, but worse, we can hear the rumbling of artillery fire in the distance – we don't know what to think.

Friday, 20th April, 1945

The Führer's birthday. How different it all is now. We are growing very uneasy. One hears of families who have left, taking just a few possessions, more are leaving now.

Saturday, 21st April, 1945

My aunt and Traute called this morning. My uncle has not returned yet – no word from him. The other families in their house are trying to get away. My aunt thought we ought to go, she thinks the Russians will be here any day. Mum is terribly worried. We are all frightened. I don't know how we can cope with aunt Anna. She is not too good on her feet. We packed in great haste, closed the door behind us and walked to the main road. There was a lot of traffic, tanks and military vehicles. They were quite willing to take us wherever they were going. We passed through the village and then lesser-known places. We just sat, numbed. After two hours we came to a stop, we had to climb down from the lorry. The soldiers asked us where we wanted to go – we had no idea. We stood there and it dawned on us – what are we doing? Who is going to house us? Feed us? Protect us? It was a mad idea! We were lucky, very lucky to find a vehicle going in the opposite direction. By the afternoon we were home again.

Sunday, 22nd April, 1945

The gunfire is much louder now. My aunt and Traute returned to us in the afternoon. At 9.00 p.m. we listened to the radio. Dr. Goebbels was speaking to the nation. "There is heroic fighting around Berlin. The Führer is near his soldiers in Berlin. We must stand fast. The new weapons will be becoming." Then the sirens announced another air-raid. We withdrew into our shelter – no sign of my uncle yet. We were five women, without a man to give us courage. There was this ominous feeling, but it can't, can't happen! Anything, but not the Russians.

An hour later there was a loud knock at the door. "Has my uncle come?" Mum went upstairs, a few moments later she was back, rushing into the room, throwing the door shut behind her.

"The Russians. The Russians!"

We stared aghast, paralysed. Then one of us moved, we must get out, get away! The window is not large, but it leads into the garden. We crawled out, we held our breath, listened. Mum and I crept behind a shrub. Where are the others? We don't know. We must not move, not make a sound! There we stayed all night until day-light broke. It was cold, our limbs ached. There was only one thought in our minds, "they must not find us."

The sun rose. It seemed safe to return to the house. We found aunt Anna, the house was untouched, but the world had changed, the world – my world – is in ruins!

The day passed, no more Russians appeared but we knew we could not carry on now. Mum is even more frightened than I am. She seems lost and helpless. Before darkness fell I had robbed my aunt of a handful of her heart pills. We swallowed them all and then with a kitchen knife we cut our wrists. It was not as easy as it had seemed but the blood flowed and we went to bed never to wake again.

Tuesday, 24th April, 1945

We are still alive! The blood no longer flowed, it was an awakening to despair! My aunt was very angry that I had taken her pills.

By midday Mum and I started our walk down to the village. It was so quiet there. Only gun fire in the distance. We walked along the empty road to our swimming pool, a former gravel pit. I had taken my swimming lessons there. I was frightened of the deep, dark water then. Now it is a different fear. They say people who can swim cannot drown! We didn't hesitate, we jumped straight in, I surfaced once, I surfaced twice – suddenly there was a rowing boat approached. Two pairs of arms, arms in Russian uniforms reached out for us, grabbed us!

We were taken across the road to the houses of local farm labourers. The Russians must have given orders that we were to be looked after. Our wet clothes were taken from us. I was put on a bed, covered with blankets. Mum was in the room next to me. I let it all happen, the hours ticked away. I knew I had to rise, see Mum, speak to her, reassure her, she was so weak. But I did not move, there was no will left, no feeling. Twenty-four hours earlier the first Russian had hammered on our door, my world collapsed, something snapped within me.

Wednesday, 25th April, 1945

Another day! Someone brought a hot drink and my dry clothes. How kind these people are, why do they bother with us? We had to leave, I went to see mum, we didn't talk, she was so weary, but we managed the long walk home.

Home seemed unreal, without meaning. Aunt Anna was not there, people around the corner appeared to have allowed her to stay; again: how good of them!

Two hours later two Russians appeared, panic gripped us, they were not menacing but came into the house, looked around and pointed to the door. We took it that we were to leave.

We crossed the road to our neighbours and sat on a bench in the garden. Only the old couple was about. The son joined the forces some months ago, after his own son, his only child, had been killed in action. The wife is an invalid, she has done nothing for months but sit in her chair. Mum has been helping her every morning and evening. She never got a "thank you" from her, nothing but moans and grumbles.

We sat in the garden, the sun was shining, it was pleasantly warm. But then another Russian appeared, came into the garden and approached us. "Come Frau," the dreaded words. We didn't move. He repeated his request more menacingly now; we shook our heads. Very slowly he took his machine-gun from his shoulder, aimed at us – we held our breath. He pulled the trigger, Mum sank down in my arms, blood trickling over my hands. I let her glide, gently, to the ground. Her eyes stared. She no longer heard me. I looked up and saw the Russian disappear through the gate. There was silence all around as I gazed at Mum. Was her life ebbing away? She did not want to live, neither of us wanted to live and now as she was so near to leaving this world, I did not want her to return to it, to this fear, this hopelessness. But I lacked the courage to help her, I could only watch.

The two old people had heard the shots. Together we carried Mum into the house and onto a bed. The bleeding was not too bad then. One shot had hit her shoulder. The other had gone through her lung. What was I to do now? Gradually she regained consciousness. I bandaged the wounds with some linen. She did not complain of pain and then night fell. Was the war still continuing? Was there fighting in Berlin? We had left it all behind, all contact was lost.

Thursday, 26th April, 1945

Another Russian soldier entered the house, how we trembled at this sight! He sat on Mum's bed, wanted to know what was wrong. He was such a nice boy, one could not hate him. He handed Mum some food – we have next to none. He was in no hurry. When at last he rose to go he turned to me with the dreaded "Frau, come." I shook my head and rushed out of the bedroom and into the kitchen, he followed, stood in the door, pulled his hand grenade, raised it high above his head, ready to throw. I drew back to the window, ready to jump. So we stood, staring at each other, for a long time, it seemed. Slowly his arm came down, he turned and went!

Poor Mum!

We really needed a doctor, but Mum would not let me out of her sight. I could not make up my mind if I should venture out, what if there were soldiers about, if they raped me, shot me?

Friday, 27th April, 1945

My aunt and Traute arrived, they had been back to their flat. They were shocked to find us in such a state. It appeared women were venturing out into the streets now, the young ones wearing old, dreary clothes and heavy scarves to disguise themselves.

My aunt insisted that we must find a doctor, there is a lady doctor living not too far from us, so we went in search of her. She came to see Mum, bandaged her wounds properly – what else could she do?

Mum pleaded with my aunt to take me with her. That put me in a terrible conflict: should I disobey my mother and insist on staying, she needs to be looked after, but the worry about me, her inability to protect me, is a terrible burden to her. If I went, was it to please my mother or was it utter selfishness? I did not know! But I went and promised to call the next day.

There is a family just down the road. A lovely family with two children, they committed suicide. The father shot them all!

My aunt is so worried about Traute and me. Much more than I at first realised. She is desperate to find a safe place for us for the night, but where? There is a lady we know who speaks Russian. When we reached her house she already had three young girls hiding in her house but she did not turn us away. We hid in the loft. Soon afterwards we heard her arguing with some Russian soldiers. She was not afraid of them, that seemed to help and they went away. We were safe for a night!

Saturday, 28ᵗʰ April, 1945

I had to keep my promise and call on Mum. I went out on my own for the first time, heavily disguised. It was all right.

On the main road I had to let a long column of German soldiers pass. They were prisoners – in their own country – their faces pale and hollow and they looked around with sad eyes. It was a horrible picture – our boys, prisoners!

I passed our bakery, there was a long queue outside. The baker has to supply the Russian troops but if any bread is left, he is allowed to hand it out to the population. No money changes hands, it is all worthless and I don't have any.

At night we begged another shelter on the loft. But in the morning our hostess implied that we could not continue coming to her house.

Sunday 29ᵗʰ April, 1945

We met a friend of my aunt's. She is well known to everybody and she offered that we could stay in the bungalow she shares with a friend. We gladly accepted. Again, we were five women coping on their own. We made up temporary sleeping places in the cellar.

After dark Russian soldiers appeared and whilst our hostess argued with them we fled into the garden. We crouched behind bushes but could not help hearing the voices from the house. She was pleading, begging – and then silence – we dared not move for hours.

It is said that the Russians had orders to behave well in Berlin – the stories that come from the East are frightening – but that is no safeguard for the women here.

Monday, 30ᵗʰ April, 1945

We dread tomorrow, the first of May. The great Socialist Holiday. We won't move out of the house.

How we wished we could have the air-raids back! They

were friendly, compared with the horror of this occupation.

Tuesday, 1st May, 1945

Tuesday, 1st May, 1945

All was quiet in the morning.

In the afternoon a group of Russians, I think, they were officers, assembled in the house. There were drinks, food and music and as the evening progressed they wanted to dance! We had no choice but the situation was full of danger. Gradually, the men grew noisy, but just as we really began to fear the worst, the senior officer broke up the party. We returned to our beds in the cellar unharmed.

Wednesday, 2nd May, 1945

I had not seen Mum for two days, so I made my way to her. Our house was still occupied, I can now see that the Russians wanted it as a temporary hospital for their wounded. If we had known, we would not have felt so bad!

In our neighbour's house there was nobody about, no Mum – what had happened?I stood in the road and looked around. On the plot next to our house there stands a tiny garden shed. I heard a noise. When I opened the door, there was our invalid neighbour, sitting on a wooden bench, all deserted and frightened – cold fear seized me. Where was Mum? She had to be somewhere! I found her with the people who had taken in aunt Anna. Mum looked ill, she was hot and feverish – I had to do something!

Thursday, 3rd May, 1945

I consulted with our hostess, she set to work. Within a few hours she had organised a stretcher and two strong men. She must also have been to our hospital – it is really no more than a sanatorium – because she had secured a bed for Mum. We lifted her onto the stretcher, covered her with blankets and the two men carried her the two kilometres through the streets to a comfortable bed and safety. I felt so grateful to those two strangers. I saw Mum settled and promised to come back soon.

Saturday, 5th May, 1945

Saturday, 5th May, 1945

My aunt and cousin have gone back to their flat and I am staying with aunt Martha and her husband. They think the cellar will be the safest place, so another bed was improvised. They treated me to a good breakfast which I accepted with a feeling of guilt but much gratitude.

We heard that in a village some distance away a farmer has harvested a field of very early potatoes and if one looks very hard one might be able to gather a few potatoes. So we shall go tomorrow.

Sunday, 6th May, 1945

It was a long walk, we found the field but there was nothing left except a few potatoes the size of marbles – many others must have visited before us.

Aunt Martha asked me to call on them before going to the hospital, she gave me a cup of soup for Mum. I had noticed that the food there was very meagre.

Mum is still feverish and very weak, but the worst was that she behaved so strangely. When I tried to help her she almost pushed me away. It made me feel uneasy and I promised to call again tomorrow.

Monday, 7th May, 1945

I slept again in the cellar. I woke during the night with a jump when something seemed to drop with a bang, but nothing stirred.

I made my way to the hospital but before I could enter the ward, a sister called me aside. Mum had died in the early hours of the morning – Mum is no more! I was left alone with her in the mortuary for a few minutes. "Good-bye, Mum. You are in peace now."

My feet carried me back to aunt Martha. There I sat on the settee, watching myself breaking the news and acting the part of a grieving daughter when inside me there was no feeling, only emptiness.

My next call had to be aunt Anna, who is still with our neighbours. Her response, "But what will happen to me now?" took me by surprise but perhaps it was understandable.

Then it was calling on my aunt and Traute.

Tuesday, 8*th* May, 1945

There are things to be done now.

An official death certificate had to be obtained, but all the authorities have disappeared. In the end I was sent to a house where the Russians together with some self-confessed Communists had set up an administration of a kind. The Russian officer laughed when I gave "shot by a Russian soldier" as the cause of death, the document now says "Pneumonia."

Then rose the question of a coffin. I heard that our local builder had been ordered to produce a large number of wooden coffins for the Russian forces. I went to see him and begged him to let me have one. He hesitated – it might get him into trouble – but he promised to help if he possibly could. His family was well known to ours.

Wednesday, 9*th* May, 1945

Now I needed transport to take Mum from the hospital to the cemetery where she would rest next to her husband. There is an old man, a local factotum, who owns a horse and cart. Most of the time he is engaged in emptying cess pools and carting the effluent to the farmers' fields. Luckily I found him and he was willing to undertake the task.

In the afternoon auntie took me for a walk into the village and then kept me waiting whilst she saw one of the church wardens. The vicar was not around, he disappeared. She made arrangements for the funeral, I didn't ask whether she paid for it.

Thursday, 10th May, 1945

We took Mum to her resting place today. There was no way I could inform any of our relatives. There are no trains – rumour has it that our retreating troops had to blow up all the bridges over the canal and the river. There is no post delivery, no telephone, nothing. They say the war ended on 8th May, one day after Mum's death!

There were just a handful of us, my aunt and Traute, aunt Martha – how good of her to come – and two other friends. Four men lowered the coffin into the grave, one of the friends spoke a few farewell words and said a prayer. I left a bunch of lilies from the garden.

Mum was only fifty – but it was a merciful end.

LIFE GOES ON

Friday, 11ᵗʰ May, 1945

It is all so futile, but I must carry on now.

I visited our house today. It is empty, but what a state it is in! The rooms are bare except for the very heavy furniture. Those of our belongings that have not disappeared are either in the garden or the cellar. The floor is covered with clothes, books, papers, household items, remains of food, chicken carcasses, blood-stained bandages – where shall I start?

We have no gas, no electricity, for water I have to use the hand-pump, no cleaning materials.

Saturday, 12ᵗʰ May, 1945

Aunt Anna had to come back. I marvel that the neighbours kept her for so long; though I think she made herself useful with mending and sewing.

There is no sewing here. All the clothes worth having have gone. I am sure the Russian soldiers did not take them. But there are now lots of Russian women going around. They were kept here in camps as foreign workers – some may even have come voluntarily – others were forced to work here. Now they are free. One cannot really blame them for helping themselves to what they fancy. Some neighbours must also have had a look for goodies, I found Mum's sewing machine some distance down the road – abandoned – so I wheeled it home again.

Tuesday, 15ᵗʰ May, 1945

We have nothing to eat and nothing to cook with. There is one small hope. When Mum decided that she wanted a gas cooker she chose one with three flames and on one side a section where one can light a fire with wood or coal. Whatever made her choose that? But we have no wood and only one box of matches which is almost empty.

I queued at the bakers for almost two hours today and came home with a loaf of bread. They say on some days the butcher has meat and he is allowed to distribute it.

Wednesday, 16th May, 1945

I went across to the small woodland at the far end of the field opposite us to gather wood. The ground was as if swept clean, I had to search for a long time to return with a bagful of twigs.

Thursday, 17th May, 1945

I am still working through the mess in the cellar. Washing in cold water, without soap – it is not very effective. But I have almost nothing to wear.

We don't hear from anybody. There is no contact with Berlin. My uncle has not yet returned. They should have allowed him home if he is still alive. And Jurgen? It is best not to think.

Friday, 18th May, 1945

I managed to secure a bag of beetroot today. Someone told me that they have a natural sugar content and make some sort of jam if boiled long enough. I sacrificed two of our precious matches and some wood – more than I wanted to – the result was awful, too awful, hungry as we are.

Saturday, 19th May, 1945

I think all my jewellery – not that I had much – has gone. I am only sorry about one necklace, the one that passed down to me from my great-grandmother.

Many of our books and photos are ruined. They are covered in dirt and blood and were trodden on.

Monday, 21st May, 1945

I did an awful thing today! I went into the bakers and

said "Heil Hitler" as I entered the shop. This was a greeting we had been encouraged to use and force of habit made me blunder. There followed a deadly silence, everybody turned round and stared at me! I was lucky nobody reported me.

Tuesday, 22nd May, 1945

There are notices up proclaiming that all former Party Members must report for work.

Wednesday, 23rd May, 1945

I reported for work.

We assembled early in the morning, after a lot of checking and more checking we were sent off to Selchow – Rudi's parents live there – to do farm work. It was a long walk and an even longer day's work. The frightening thing was that the Russian soldiers were around us all day and we don't trust them. We tried to stay together in groups as a kind of protection. But we were fed well with a good stew – Barsch – at lunchtime. Barsch is vegetables cooked with all kinds of meat, the richer the better. Ours was probably not the richest. I did not arrive home again until very late, but as our clocks are adjusted to Russian time – though every parish has its different adjustment of time – we still have daylight at 11.00 p.m.

Sunday, 27th May, 1945

Our daily march to work is pretty tiring. I called on Rudi's house. Only his mother is at home, she is having a tough time.

It appears that I shall soon be allowed to work in our own village.

Saturday, 2nd June, 1945

Some people think that life is returning slowly to normal but there is nothing normal about it. No food, no money, no gas, no electricity, no mail, no news, no trains, hardly any clothes only the sun is shining and it is warm.

The Russian soldiers are so primitive. Not only do they go around wearing a dozen watches on their arms (they never had any before,) one can observe them in the streets learning to ride a bicycle and I have seen them washing vegetable in the toilet basin!

Eileen came today to ask if I could offer her family a roof over their heads, they were made to leave their flat. She has two children, the youngest is only four months old. It must be terrible for a mother! Of course they can come!

8*th* June, 1945

Eileen's family has been with us only a few days, but this morning two men came to the door and asked for her husband, I called him and left him to speak to them. A few minutes later I saw all three walking towards the next street and I noticed a car was standing there. Eileen has not seen her husband since, it is very eerie!

18*th* June, 1945

Auntie and Eileen are not getting on too well but Eileen spends most of the day with her mother-in-law. I work in the village now. I know the family quite well and they all knew Mum. We are out in the fields all day. The farmers here specialise in vegetables for the Berliner market. There are early lettuce and radishes – I took a bagful home, not much of a meal but something edible.

The farmers don't starve but nearly all the farm animals have gone, taken by the Russians. I suppose as victors they are entitled to take what they need.

ARREST

Thursday, 21ˢᵗ June, 1945

It was almost lunchtime when someone from the farm came to call me. Two men were asking for me. They said the Russian Commandant wanted to speak to me and would I come with them? So I washed my hands and went. It was a long walk from the village, past our house, through the railway tunnel and onto the house which is now the Commandant's headquarters. My two guardians tried to be friendly and make conversation.

The Commandant – quite an imposing figure – asked a lot of questions and then demanded to see documents. Of course, I had none. So he ordered me into his car and drove me home.

I went through the motion of looking for papers, but I knew there was nothing to be found, nothing relating to any political activities. He gave up in the end but said that I had to come with him again.

I asked, "For how long?"

He shrugged his shoulders and said, "A day or two."

There was just time to push a comb and a toothbrush into a small bag, grab my light summer coat (I loved that coat even though it was long past its prime) and as an afterthought I tucked a blanket (it had served as a black-out for one of our windows for years) under my arm.

Auntie had been looking on all the time with some consternation – there was not much time for a "Good-bye."

As we walked back to the car the officer said "Did Hitler marry Eva Braun?" I looked at him in amazement. I had never heard of an Eva Braun? Who was she? And the Führer marry! The thought had never entered my mind.

On the way back to the headquarters the car passed my aunt and Traute, but they did not see me and I did not dare wave to them.

There was a lorry waiting outside the headquarters,

twenty men already loaded onto it. I was made to join them, the only woman. I vaguely knew some of the men.

We drove off, soon the villages were no longer familiar. Our journey ended outside a biggish house, from what we could gather we were in Koenigswusterhausen.

The men had their pockets turned out, the contents went flying onto a big heap, then they were led away. I was left on a seat in the front garden.

There I remained for hours!

Friday, 22nd June, 1945

It must have been about 9.00 p.m. last night when I was marched into the house and a room where three Russian officers and a female interpreter were waiting. I soon realised that she was not a good interpreter.

Questions were fired at me.

"Were you a member of Hitler's Party?" "Yes."

"When did you join?" "1942."

"Where did you go to school?" "Berlin."

"What sort of school?" "Grammar school."

"What is a Grammar School?" "A school where one learns languages." I answered, not able to think of a better description.

"What languages?" "English and French."

"Ah! You a spy!" I wish I had not said that.

"Where did you work?" "Kanzlei des Führers."

Surprisingly, no special reaction.

"Where were you the last few months?" "In anti-aircraft units."

"You told to fight Russian army!" "No."

"Commandant says you fight Russians, you Werewolf." "No, no."

So we went on.

There followed a pause, I was led into the basement. The rooms down there were all occupied by dozens of men. I was left standing next to the sentry who was guarding us all. He smoked, and to my horror the men, our German men, begged for the cigarette ends! I felt ashamed.

At midnight a section of a mattress appeared and was put on the floor just where I stood and I was motioned to lie down for the night. I did and I slept. I was beyond caring.

Saturday, 23rd June, 1945

It must have been in the early hours of the morning when I was woken and marched upstairs to the interrogation room. It was a long session. Always the same questions, the same answers, only once did I make a mistake by giving a different date and was immediately pulled up over that. Mental note: don't contradict yourself, don't lie.

When we came to the end of the questions, another officer appeared, another interpreter and off we went again.

"You had orders to fight the Russian army!"

Again and again my answer was "No." I felt so frustrated and angry tears welled up in my eyes.

"I am telling the truth, I am not a liar!"

In the end a document was produced and put in front of me. All I could see was that the last two paragraphs were written in Russian. A pen was pushed into my hand. "Sign here." There was no point in arguing, even if it was my death sentence, so I signed.

I returned to my mattress which was withdrawn at 6.00 a.m.

Then something ridiculous happened: four soldiers with guns over their shoulders appeared and marched me out of the house and into the remoter part of the garden ... ... where a washbasin waited for me! Supervised by four guns I attended to my morning toilet!

Later in the morning it was back onto the lorry. There were far more men now, we were tightly packed. A few optimists expressed the view that we were on the way home. "Two days," the Officer had said.

No. It was not the journey home. Just a transfer to

another place, another building.

I found myself locked into a large room surrounded by men, but that appeared a mistake.

But my misfortune was to have to share a room with twenty Russian girls. Why are they here? Some were ethnic Germans who had lived for generations in Russia, had then opted to return to Germany and now that things had gone wrong, were siding with the Russians again. But the authorities took a poor view of this and locked them up together with those Russian women who had worked in Germany – forced or voluntarily.

My roommates displayed quite a wardrobe of pretty dresses and they spent the afternoon trying on and swapping, applying make-up and altogether enjoying themselves.

In the evening we lined up outside for counting – the men looked dreadful, unshaven and unhappy. The Russian girls stood in one group, posing in their finery. I kept a step apart. In my threadbare skirt and flimsy blouse – when did I last have a perm? I saw our men looking across to me and I suddenly felt proud and I smiled encouragement back at them.

Sunday, 24ᵗʰ June, 1945

What a night that was! There are two-tier bunk beds in our room. I had one of the lower ones. When darkness fell our room came to life! Though we were locked in it was obviously all right for the sentries to visit. The pretty dresses and painted lips had done their work! The laughing and shrieking and banging went on for hours.

At midday food arrived. A bowl of very watery soup for me and a large container of a rich stew for the others. When they all had their fill, one of the Russians handed me a spoon and pointed at the leftovers. Of course I could not resist a decent meal.

The evening concluded with more counting.

Monday, 25th June, 1945

Another wild night. I was too tired to keep awake, as long as nobody touched me … …

As the morning progressed I wished I had resisted the rich food. I had awful diarrhoea and we were locked in and only allowed out at certain times. I banged at the door but the sentries didn't or didn't want to hear. It was very distressing.

Tuesday, 26th June, 1945

This morning we were told to get ready, great urgency was implied. The Russian girls grabbed what appeared most precious to them but a lot of 'their' belongings were left behind in a heap. I spotted a large, linen sheet, I knew this was too good to be disregarded, I lingered a little and when the last of the Russians was about to leave the room I pointed at the sheets and said "I will take that."

She nodded and went on, I grabbed my treasure and followed.

A voice inside me reminded me that I should have been too proud to beg, but … … was it begging?

Another lorry journey – a convoy of lorries – a drive through the summer countryside – until a gate, a wide, solid gate opened and closed behind us.

CONCENTRATION CAMPS

(i)   Ketschendorf

Tuesday, 26th June, 1945

This is Ketschendorf, near Fuerstenwalde.

One might think we have come to a small town, streets lined with semi-detached, two-storey houses, gardens behind them, taller houses, a block of flats. But there are no happy families living here, barbed-wire separates the houses and in the distance one becomes aware of sentry towers all around.

A woman, a German woman – what a relief – greeted me and led me into one of the houses and a ground floor room. I stared in amazement. There were twenty women in that room, measuring no more than 3 metres by 4 metres and not a single item of furniture in it!

It appears this camp was established in May and has been filling up ever since, probably to several thousand people.

I soon learnt that the day here comprises two main events. Being counted and waiting for food.

Counting happens twice a day. The call from the sentry gets everybody up and out of the house for the roll-call. We line up three deep and wait until the Russian officer arrives and counts us. The German Commandant (a prisoner like us) then counts and then the interpreter counts and if the figures don't tally, they all return and count again.

Food is received three times a day. After the shout "Kubeltrager raus" two representatives from every block go to the kitchen and return with our morning coffee, i.e. hot water with which we also receive a portion of very damp bread. At lunchtime it is soup – warm water in which a few oats are floating. This is repeated in the evening, more warm water but instead of oats a few small cubes of potato and even fewer of meat are visible.

The evening meal was my first encounter with this ritual. No receptacles are provided. One has to improvise. Anything goes: saucepans, tins, plates, only jars are to be avoided, their bottoms fall out! I was lucky again, a kind soul handed me a bowl.

When it came to sleeping time – one cannot call it bed time, as there are no beds – we all went down onto the floor, half of us head one side of the room, the other half facing the opposite direction, the legs overlap in the middle. How very lucky I am having a blanket to lie on and a coat to spread over me!

During the night we are allowed to use the toilet upstairs. During the day we go to the loo at the end of the garden. This is a wooden structure, almost ten metres long, erected over a fairly deep ditch. In front of this hole runs a beam on which one squats – no privacy there!

The morning wash is dealt with in the bathroom upstairs, but there is little water, no soap, but I am rich, I own a toothbrush and a flannel.

When it is time to receive our daily bread, someone has to assume the terrible responsibility of cutting a loaf into perfectly equal portions of 300 gr. each – this is to last us for the day. I noticed that most of the women eat the lot immediately. It will require great willpower to keep some for later in the day, or even for a few hours, we are all so hungry.

Early July, 1945

I have joined the group of women who go over to the kitchen every day to peel potatoes. We sit in the open and peel! The potatoes are not very good and the more we cut away, the thinner the soup will be for the thousands of hungry people. I don't think we are supposed to, but I ate a few raw potatoes. Some of the women use this job to talk to the men in the kitchen to enquire – not allowed of course – about relatives or friends.

There is a woman in my room who is sewing for the Russian officers and their families. She took my piece of linen and I now have two pairs of pants and two left-overs which will serve as towels – I am very rich indeed! I paid her by allowing her to use part of the material for herself.

Mid July, 1945

I am now working in the 'hospital' and I am very grateful. Sitting around all day is dreadful, one cannot forget the hunger.

The so-called hospital is in the larger building and we are escorted there every morning and back at night.

Conditions in the hospital are dreadful and so is the smell. The men lie on wooden benches, but we have no mattresses, no blankets, no spare clothes, no medication, no extra food. Most of the men are so weak, we can offer them nothing but comforting words.

My particular charges are four men who are kept in isolation, they have a room to themselves which they are not allowed to leave, but I go in and out without any protection. I have not asked what is wrong with them. One of them talks a lot, he is very angry. He says he was an opera singer but because he is half-Jewish he was never allowed to perform. When the war ended he went to the authorities and claimed compensation and now he is here! He thinks he will soon be free because it is obviously a mistake that he is locked up. It is an ironical situation but I suppose he became a nuisance to the Russian authorities and they got rid of him. They are obviously not very fussy as to who disappears into these camps.

I am sure now that the Russians don't care who they lock up – they don't have to prove a case against us. They probably have a target figure of X numbers of thousands and to them all Germans are guilty and they are correct in their way. We all supported the war and the Government that started it, at least nobody actively opposed it.

End July, 1945

One of the girls who works as a nurse is a French girl. She is very beautiful. They say she was engaged to a German officer and when the war ended she made her way to Germany in search of her fiancé – until the Russians arrested her.

The other nurse is Marlis, she is a wonderful person, full of confidence, courage and compassion.

It is dreadful to see these sick men, they look to us for comfort and hope. Strange, that so many men see in us the stronger beings, the more able to cope, yet the Russians allow us no privileges.

Dysentery is the biggest problem. Yet all we can do is stop the men from eating the damp bread. We toast it for them over the fire which we are allowed to keep in the kitchen but it is far too hot and burns the bread.

We are fighting for the life of a young boy – he is fifteen or sixteen – the youngest in the camp is twelve. He was playing Werewolf in the street. Marlis is determined he will not die, but he does not help, he will eat anything he can reach, he is so hungry.

Every morning we find one or two of the men missing. A black paper bag and a mass grave is all there is for them – and their families at home are waiting for them.

We have three doctors, all fellow prisoners. One is a very charming young doctor from Vienna – but what can they do?

I spoke to a man who admitted to having been a communist all his life but is now so disgusted that he has changed his belief.

Marlis has presented me with a small, black scarf which I now use to tie up my hair, it was so thoughtful of her. We must look awful, bony and in rags, glad there are no mirrors about.

August, 1945

The Russians are obsessed with cleanliness. There is a female officer going around, inspecting our rooms. If the floor is not wet, she will chase us to find buckets and a brush. The dampness is no good to anybody, the floors never dry out.

There is a wonderful old man here in the hospital. Perhaps he isn't all that old. He is not quite as ill as most of the others and he has taken on the job of washing the filthy trousers of his comrades. Yet they say he owned a factory and is here because the Russians would not believe that he was not a member of Hitler's party. He is a tonic to us all with his smile and his patience.

I find working rather hard now, my legs are very swollen and heavy.

A Few Days Later

Yesterday I was ordered to stop working. The young doctor was coming up a flight of stairs behind me, my legs were so heavy I had to pull myself up on the railings. He saw it and sent me back to my quarters.

Today I have been sitting in the garden, enjoying the sun, but every time I had to get up to walk down to the loo, which happened often, my foot was hurting terribly.

I mentioned it later to a couple of my room mates when they returned from the hospital. They appeared to be very worried and late in the evening I was carried back to the hospital – as a patient. I am in an isolation room, nobody says why.

Two Days Later

Yesterday someone from my room sent me a tiny sprig of a weed, found in the garden behind our house (very few grow because they are all picked before they have a chance.) I chopped it and sprinkled it on that pint of water soup – it was such a treat!

Another Two Days Gone

I am much better now and out of the isolation room. In the bed opposite me is a young girl, she looks so very young and she is too weak to leave her bunk. Her body is covered in bed sores but she never complains, though she must be in great pain. I think she knows that she will not recover – she is a saint!

In the evenings I give a hand in the small kitchen. It is very hot in there. Last night I happened to be alone in the kitchen when the young doctor came in. We talked for a few minutes and then he suddenly kissed me! It was my first kiss but he will never know that – and I fainted!

Next Day

This morning the doctor did his round and, urgently requiring space for others, sent me back to my room!

We are always being moved about, new people arrive, some in small groups, some in very large numbers. Through the newcomers we hear from the world outside the camp. Ketschendorf is known as a Schweigelager (silent camp). There is no contact between us inside these fences and the outside world.

Some women suffer terribly from being locked up here. They have parents, husbands or children outside. There is one woman here who was arrested in the street and her small child handed to a passer-by.

I consider myself fortunate. I know my mother is at rest and aunts and cousins have their own sorrows and worries and will have got over the shock of my disappearance.

But to some this suffering is affecting their health and this is made far worse by the many rumours that are passed from mouth to mouth. I almost believe they are deliberately started by the Russians. This clinging to hope which is then dashed when the days go by and we are still here.

I am immune to all these whispered promises of going home soon. I neither believe nor disbelieve them.

There is a story told that a Russian officer said, "We nix bang, bang, you lots of soup, soup and more soup and then you fat legs and *kaput*". There is method in all this!

Newcomers brought the news that there was a conference of the four Allies held in Potsdam and that Germany is now divided into four parts and that Berlin, as our capital, has also been divided into four sections, one occupied by the Americans, British, French or Russians. My home town must now belong to the Russians.

September, 1945

Bunk beds have been put into our rooms. They are roughly made and without mattress or even straw to cover the wooden planks on which we now sleep.

When we are taken to our weekly showers, we have to hand in all our clothes for disinfecting – because we suffer from lice and fleas. Whilst we wait, naked, we have to parade past a doctor for inspection – one loses all shame and need for privacy. When our clothes come back they are warm out of the oven. For how long will those flimsy, over-used clothes last before they fall to pieces?

I am not feeling very strong these days. I have a big boil on my face and now a few more under my arm. When I went to the bathroom yesterday morning and lifted my arm the pus ran out as if I had turned on a tap. I am told such boils are very weakening – I feel it too.

Two days ago the women who carry our lunchtime soup from the kitchen had an accident and dropped the lot just as they reached our houses, which meant half ration for all of us. I could not stop myself from getting down on my knees to pick up the few cubes of potato and meat that were left on the ground – the 'soup' had no difficulty in disappearing into the soil! I felt ashamed of myself!

October, 1945

Standing outside for the twice daily roll-call is becoming very unpleasant. Not only because I have twice fainted when we had to be counted and recounted (there are a few hundred of us now) but more so because our summer clothes are totally inadequate in this cold weather – I don't even have stockings.

A baby was born here recently, everybody was sure the mother would be allowed home. But no! A lot of women try to help the young mother, but what a way to start life for the poor little thing.

November, 1945

I have no go in me. I spend all day resting on those boards called our beds. A very nice woman has moved into our room, we all call her Aunt Sophie. She is a tall, well-built woman. She held a fairly high position in the Red Cross in Berlin – what a crime! She takes a very motherly interest in me and has insisted that the doctor must come and see me. He did and brought his stethoscope!

We all fear the winter and Christmas is entering into our thoughts. So many cling to the hope that we must be home by then. The Russian officers say so too!

December, 1945

There is an iron stove in one corner of our room. Our allocation of fuel is two small pieces of wood per day. The fire does not last long. We are beginning to look around for additional supplies, one or two planks from our beds have already been sacrificed.

The nights are an ordeal now for me. My legs are still very swollen. It is retained fluids in the body. This is a major cause of death in the camp, as the officer said, "soup, soup and then *kaput*." I saw men in the hospital, their legs were so fat, they could no longer take their trousers off and the water rises and when it reaches the heart ... ... they simply drown.

I am lucky: when I lie down at night the water seems to gravitate down and I have to go to the toilet five or six times a night. But now I perspire so much, I wake up wet around my chest. So I try to dry myself with my 'towel', go upstairs into the cold bathroom and after that it takes a long time to get back into my one blanket. I lie on half of it and the other half I try to pull over my body, tucking it in carefully to keep out the cold air. Once all this has been achieved it is almost necessary to start again.

Muttchen has moved into our room. She still wears her cotton dress but she has lost a lot of weight! She comes from a small town near the Oder. She is the type of woman everybody would seek out for advice and leadership. She ran the '*Frauenschaft*', the official organisation for women. From her I received a pair of men's long-johns. There are only two ways of acquiring additional clothes or anything else. With contacts one might obtain clothes taken from those who died, or one has to pay with a number of bread portions – which is very hard.

24th December, 1945

24th December, 1945

It is Christmas Eve! All those reassurances of going home have come to nothing. Nobody mentions Christmas now, but we all have our thoughts.

I wandered out into the garden and looked up into the star-lit sky. What will Christmas be at home? Are they, too, starving? For a few moments the sound of "Silent Night, Holy Night" flickered through my mind. "No, it is no good." I went back into our dreary, cold, over-crowded room.

January, 1946

Muttchen had to stop working in the hospital. She is not well. She looks ill, very ill. She must be in her fifties, she was used to healthy country life – it is hard for her. I have given her my coat for the night, it is not much.

It is very cold. Even the lavatory seats have been dismantled and turned into firewood.

There is a woman here whose crime was enquiring after her son. About a dozen boys disappeared from the same small town. They had been playing Werewolf! The Russians seem to be very touchy on that subject. The mother did not stop asking questions. When a Swiss organisation took up her case, the mother disappeared!

February, 1946

What made me do it? I stood by Muttchen's bedside today – she occupies one of the upper bunks – and told her my story. Our attempted suicide, Mum's death and how I came to be here. It all just poured out, everybody must have been listening, but I didn't notice.

We are all obsessed by food, people sit together in small groups and exchange recipes. We are not allowed to have knives, scissors, needles, pencils or paper in our possession.

Every now and then the Russians surprise us with a 'razzia'. We have to remain outside and they go from house to house turning everything inside out looking for forbidden items. Some women do own one or other of these prohibited treasures and the thought of losing them causes anxiety. One takes a great risk writing down precious recipes which are meant to be tried out when home again.

I understand the men, too, are gripped by this disease. How low one sinks when the body is starving!

Story-telling has become a welcome diversion, of course, it is not allowed. A few women have wonderful memories, they can sit down and relate in great details books they read many years ago. We lie on our bunks and escape into another world.

March, 1946

I am feeling better, not perspiring so much. The doctors are worried about our malnutrition and they have hit on an idea of giving us pine needle tea and the authorities have agreed to it. Whole pine trees are brought into the camp, working parties spend the day extracting the needles and from them tea is brewed and distributed every morning. The taste is awful, I hold my nose and gulp it down quickly.

Feeling stronger, I have to take my turn on sentry duties. Day and night every house has to have someone on duty at the door. Only during the worse winter months are we allowed to remain inside the door whilst on night duty. All this hardship just the please the Russians. We stand to attention when they walk past.

During my early morning shift I saw, for the first time, the wagon pulled by weary men. They come from the hospital and slowly make their way towards the main gate. This wagon carries the night's dead to their mass grave. Word has it that there are forty dead every night, that makes four hundred in ten days, one thousand two hundred in a month. There are about twelve thousand people in this camp now – so we shall all be dead in ten months! Of course, this will not happen, the numbers are always made up by new arrivals.

April, 1946

We are now so overcrowded we sleep two to a bunk. That is two on the upper bunk and two on the lower. We are packed in like sardines. One cannot move without disturbing the other person, yet one has to move frequently because we are all badly bruised from sleeping on the bare boards. The only benefit is, we keep each other warm.

Two girls from another house have been taken ill and are being looked after in a room nobody else is allowed to enter. Diphtheria is talked about – it could be very serious for all of us. There is no medication for them – they gargle – with their own urine!

May, 1946

The trees in the garden are turning green – one tiny sign of hope.

Some sort of craze has spread through our houses. We are holding séances. It is quite simple. On a board (taken from a bed) the letters of the alphabet are written in a circle, on one corner the words 'yes' and 'no' and at the other end the figures 0 to 9. Also required is an upturned saucer with an indicator marked in one place. Three of us sit around the board, hands lightly placed on the saucer with thumbs and little fingers touching. The woman who leads the séance then calls on the spirit of a departed and asks him if he will answer our questions. He usually points at the 'yes' and we proceed. Only when Muttchen is one of the participants nothing happens (she is too down to earth.) We take it in turn to put our questions and the saucer moves about spelling out the answers. I was very sceptical until I asked "Who lives now in my house?" The plate started moving and I followed its darting about with interest, to my amazement, it spelled G R O N E R T; the name of my aunt and cousin who lived in their flat when I disappeared. The name was certainly not on my mind when I asked the question and nobody here ever heard me mention names of my relatives – very strange!

The diphtheria girls are recovering but they have lost all their hair; one used to be in my room, she has a lovely voice.

June, 1946

I was the talk of the camp yesterday. I was taken out through the big gate. As far as I remember this happened only once before when Marianne and her mother were escorted out. If anyone thought that I went into freedom, such thoughts never occurred to me.

I was taken into an office where a uniformed man started questioning me. It was all about the Reichstag and it took me a little while to convince him that I knew nothing about the Reichstag (they obviously confused it with the Reichskanzlei, a different building.) I suppose to cover up for this mistake he asked if I had been a member of the Party. I admitted that I was and he retorted, "All Germans say 'no' not Party member."

I felt ashamed again, why are we feeling so superior when times are good and turn into cowards when we are down? The officer spoke German very well, the conversation became light-hearted.

"Did you see Hitler?" I nodded confirmation.

"How many times?" I thought quickly and decided on a slightly lower estimate. "Six times."

"You stay here six years then!" He smiled. I smiled back. End of interview!

It is a year since I arrived here – a whole year!

July, 1946

In a cellar room below us lives a girl, locked up, she lost her reason. Sometimes she screams, sometimes she recites poetry. Someone is with her all the time to calm her down and stop her from harming herself. I believe she held a senior position in the Hitler Youth. Her screaming and howling is eerie.

The Russian girls who arrived with me, and many others, have left. There was a very attractive, very proud, girl among them. I heard she was a parachutist and was being punished for allowing herself to be taken prisoner by us. These girls did not want to return to Russia, they did not expect ever to be free again in their own country. They went without all the goodies they had assembled in Germany. Stalin would not let anybody bring back evidence of our much higher standard of living.

August, 1946.

The Russians, especially their wives, get a lot of unpaid labour out of us.

I have just spent two days working for a family. I was taken out of the camp and returned in the afternoon. It is a prized occupation as one receives an extra helping of watery soup but more importantly, the family feeds one during the day. I had to do cleaning jobs and look after a child. I hated it! Obviously, I was not popular and soon released!

The Russian women also send their washing in. Three of us are working almost day and night. They boil the clothes in one of the cellar rooms in a copper kettle. Initially they were allowed two days, now the dirty clothes arrive in the afternoon and are collected, clean, dry and ironed in the morning. This means our women work all night in that hot, damp, airless room, drying the clothes near a roaring fire – it is very unhealthy – all for a bit of extra food!

August, 1946

There is an American woman here. Ilse-Veda, she was a concert violinist. Her husband, a German, held a senior position in the Propaganda Ministry. When the Russians arrested him, she used her American Citizenship to demand his release. Now she is here, she is quite elderly, though she won't disclose her age to anyone. She is very eccentric and nobody can get on with her. I feel very sorry for her. We all suffer but it must be harder for a person who was used to comfort and admiration. She insists she must have warm water in the morning to wash her face and hands (her hands are precious to her.) She made arrangements somehow and I volunteered to act as her 'water carrier'.

A group of women left the camp a few weeks ago. Now the story is circulating that before their departure they promised to return to a distant spot which can be seen from the camp and wave to show that they are free. They have now been seen and there is much excitement.

September, 1946

I am so upset, no. Outraged!

We were all marched off and lined up in a square and after a long wait the Russian Commandant appeared and, through an interpreter, informed us that a few youngsters had been caught stealing and as punishment they would be going to Siberia. What had happened was that a lorry, loaded with clothes, had come into the camp and a working party, including these boys, were unloading when the boys, who are still wearing their thin summer shirts, took a few clothes for themselves and probably another item for a friend, and they were caught in the act. These boys are hungry and cold and now they go to Siberia!

October, 1946

Our beds are riddled with bed bugs! I am lucky, they don't like me, but it is dreadful, they crawl all over the beds at night. We try to burn them out; we go all over the bunks with a burning piece of wood. So far the place has not gone up in flames, not yet!

I have not seen myself in a mirror for eighteen months but I know I am terribly thin. I used to be plump, but now I am as flat as a board, only the hip bones and ribs sticking out. When I put my thumb and middle finger around my upper arm, they touch.

November, 1946

A woman in our room brought in a handful of potatoes, which we are, of course, not to have but she has contacts with people on work commands. She boiled them when the fire in our stove was hot. There were many envious eyes, but she could not share with twenty others. However, I received the potato water and I thought it tasted delicious. When I am home, I will never again throw away potato water.

December, 1946

Another winter is upon us – I don't know whether to believe or not that we shall ever be free again.

When our shoes wear out, we wrap rags around our feet

Another Christmas is coming – it is terrible to see how

some people suffer. It only takes one rumour and for days they live in ecstasy of hope and then they are right down!

January, 1947

It has turned bitterly cold, the frost is very severe. The camp is buzzing with rumours. There is a restlessness about. Everybody is sure something big is going to happen. Some people think the Russians are just waiting for the weather to improve.

18ᵗʰ January, 1947

Early this morning it happened! We were to pack our belongings – not much to pack. For some time now I have owned a bag, a piece of brown material stitched together on both sides and held by two wooden sticks on the top. At night it has served me as a pillow, after I put my other possessions into it. That and my blanket are my luggage.

We stood outside in that cold weather and waited and were counted and counted again and then the march began, out of the gate and on over a flat, deserted landscape. It did not feel like freedom. The weak stumbled and tried desperately to keep up with the rest. What fate was there for those who fell behind? And then we saw the train! A long goods train, waiting for us in the cold, bleak countryside!

(ii)   Jamlitz

18ᵗʰ January, 1947

In groups of fifty we were ordered, with shouting and pushing, into the wagons. We helped each other reach the opening which was well above the ground and then the doors closed behind us and a lock was turned. Inside it was dark, cold and dirty. I couldn't see but it felt as if coals had been transported in it recently. I found a sack or something like it to sit on and wrapped my blanket around me. So we sat for a long time until eventually the noise outside died down. I must have dropped off to sleep, the train was moving when I woke.

19ᵗʰ January, 1947

We have been in this dark hole for more than twenty-four hours. During the night, when the train had stopped, the doors were flung open, loaves of bread were handed in and the door closed again. Again the problem arose how to cut each loaf into seven and half portions. All day long the train moved, stopped and reversed, we had no idea where it was taking us.

There was a loo of a kind in one corner, it needed emptying when the train stopped.

Now we are spending a second night locked up in this travelling prison – there is a woman on the train about to give birth!

There occurred a great commotion. The doors were pushed open, the guards shouted, we didn't understand a word. Apparently, a piece of paper had been found with a message written on it. The guards assumed that it had been dropped from the train and the culprit had to be found. There were threats of heavy punishment. I don't think anybody was caught – but a warning it was. It is not for nothing that we are a 'silent camp'.

21st January, 1947

My birthday!

Early in the morning the train stopped once again. Something seemed to happen. The door opened "dawai," "dawai" – quickly. We blinked into the daylight from our dark prison, we saw snow on the ground. The train had stopped at a country station 'Lieberose' and there were trees, lots of them, around it.

Word went around that near here was Jamlitz, a former concentration camp for the Jews. Some even claimed that it was known as an Interim Camp, one stop from freedom. It did not feel like that.

It took ages to get everybody off the train and into formation but then, surprisingly, our destination was not far from the railway station.

We marched through the gate. My first impression was how small it seemed and how crammed it was. Fences and barbed wire everywhere. Also a few wooden huts and snow piled high.

The worst impression was the sight of a group of men standing motionless, skeletons in rags, rough beards hiding hollow cheeks and eyes that stared at us, eyes without life. Did they pity us or were they beyond caring? I will never forget those ghostly appearances.

After endless waiting and counting – it was still bitterly cold – we were taken into our new 'homes'. What a shock! We had lived in cramped conditions in Ketschendorf, but these were badly built huts with three-storey bunks along the walls and also filling the whole area, reaching from floor to ceiling leaving just narrow passages between. Several hundred women crowded into this one room, each one grabbing a space on a bunk. The older women made for the lowest tier. Erni, a girl I had spoken to in Ketschendorf, pulled me along and sent me up to the top tier. There was just sufficient room for four to sleep side by side on an area about three metres square and with headroom to sit, but not to stand up. Again, it was just bare boards, no mattresses, no blankets.

22nd *January, 1947*

The food here is as awful, or worse than before. The 'soup' is a greyish-blue water with a few oats swimming in it.

The building is terribly draughty and it looks as if there is nothing for us to do but to stretch out on our narrow strip of boarding. It is a horribly dark, cold, inhuman place.

23rd *January, 1947*

It is strange. We seem to have formed a little unit, the four of us. Erni is from Berlin, a lovely girl. I am sure we will become real friends. She was not politically active but her job has got her into trouble. Then we have Mulle, a sweet, little girl, very pretty, with a lovely smile. She was taken by the Russians when her friend and friend's mother were arrested. Our number four is Edelgard, she arrived in Ketschendorf much later than we did, at a time when the Russians had rounded up all the Party Members, real or imagined, and were locking up people who proved a nuisance to them. Her arrest had something to do with crossing the East-West frontier. From all we hear, there is a marked difference between the parts of Germany that are occupied by the Western forces and the one the Russians now hold. Edelgard is a bit of a mystery, but we get on very well.

February, 1947

It is still so very cold. Apart from the daily counting and trips to the loo – which is outside the hut – we sit on our bunks.

We have four stoves in the hut but they are useless. The first heating session starts at 4.00 a.m. As soon as the fire is burning smoke begins to fill the room and the order comes to extinguish the fire and to open the doors (there are no windows.) This sequence is repeated three times a day.

In addition we have visits from the Russians who come to inspect and always find reasons for ordering the scrubbing of the floor and then we have a damp room. It is quite ridiculous.

One thing is very different here, as the camp is so small, we are much nearer to the men's compound. When we are taken for our shower – once in a while – (the same dreary affair, too little water, no soap, no towels and not much time) we walk past some of the men. A few of our women know that their husbands were taken by the Russians and they strain their eyes and sometimes call out their names. One of them has actually found her husband and has waved to him from a distance.

March, 1947

Mulle's birthday is near and we have plans! Every day we keep a thin slice of bread which we dry or toast on the stove, if we can get near it and when it is hot.

Our daily food ration also includes a teaspoon of butter and jam, and of this, too, we save a little. The idea is that we can produce a cake for the birthday – we will crush the toast and mix it with the butter and jam so that it will form into a cake.

It is a wonderful idea, something to think about and look forward to. When did we last look forward to anything? Perhaps warmer weather, which brings so much relief.

31ˢᵗ March, 1947

The snow is beginning to thaw, though there are still mountains of it outside the huts. The midday sun brings some warmth.

3ʳᵈ April, 1947

This morning it was 'packing' again and standing in the open air, waiting to be counted and our names to be called.

Then the march through the gate. Thankfully, it was a short march to the station where the goods train was waiting – all so familiar now. We must be nearly a thousand women.

Again, it was an empty, dark, cold wagon where we sat and waited. Word went round that a young girl among us came from this little town and that the German station master had recognised her. When the train started moving she sat with her eyes glued to a narrow gap in the wall and at a level crossing she saw her mother standing there. Her cry "Mammie" went through every fibre of my body and as the train rambled on and stopped and reversed, I hid my head under my blanket and cried and cried.

(iii)   Muhlberg

Here we are: Muhlberg!

For almost two nights and two days we were locked into darkness, no place to sit, no place to lie down, nowhere to wash. Just the customary opening of doors during the night when food was pushed into our hands.

When the doors opened this morning we looked out into a wide, flat, bleak landscape. Not a house or tree in sight. I did not realise there were such bleak places in Germany.

We had to jump out of the wagon, difficult even for young legs after forty-eight hours or being crammed into a dark space, dangerous for the old and weak. And then the long march began, hundreds of weary figures stumbling towards another prison.

When we passed through the gates we seemed to have entered into a primitive village. There was a long, straight road and wooden huts on either side. Only the barbed wire fences between the buildings made it very different. After Jamlitz there is so much space!

After hours of waiting and, surprise, surprise, more counting, we were at last marched into our new quarters.

How does one react to such a barn of a place? It is about thirty metres long and ten metres wide and very high, seven or eight metres. All around the walls run two wooden galleries, one just above the ground, the other well above that, reached via a ladder. That is where we are going to live!

There is one thing which makes me very happy. During the transport I lost sight of my three friends but somehow we found each other again. Edelgard secured a very good place for us, on the upper gallery and the inside wall.

We discovered that behind us is the washroom – concrete troughs with a few cold water taps and beyond that room is another identical one to ours, each housing over two hundred women.

Again we sleep on the bare boards, but I suppose we shall sleep tonight!

6th April, 1947

There are advantages here: the food is served inside our room and not in the open. It is still the same watery soup and a portion of bread plus the occasional teaspoon of butter, sugar or jam.

In front of our 'barn' is a large, open space, almost like a parade ground and beyond that is the 'old camp'. Smaller huts occupied by a few hundred women who have been living here for some time.

We also discovered a sunken pond, quite a sizeable one. The prospect for the summer is not bad.

Strange, that I can find so much that is positive. The world outside is almost unreal now. It is here that we live and if we can't adapt we go under. We talk of going home but I almost feel that some of the older women are afraid of it. Will their husbands, their children, be waiting for them? What if they find themselves alone and unable to provide for themselves?

Late April, 1947

These buildings are terribly draughty. The wind blows through the gaps and the only means of heating the place are most peculiar. A low brick structure at each end of the room and a built-in pipe connecting the two. If a fire is lit they spread a little warmth, if one keeps near to them. But the wide open space will never get warm – a bad prospect for the winter.

May, 1947

I saw Mrs. Bechler the other day, the woman everybody talks about. She is a very attractive person with an air of reserve about her. The story goes that her husband was an army officer who was taken prisoner by the Russians and joined the Paulus Army that fought with the Russians. We never believed that German officers could do such a thing. Her husband is now said to be in Eastern Germany, holding a position of Minister of the Interior in the land of Brandenburg and is married again. He obviously had his wife dumped here so that he was free from reminders of the past. What a dreadful fate for her!

Early July, 1947

The Russian authorities keep out of sight here. The camp has so far been run by a very unpopular man, Haller, of course a prisoner like the rest of us. But he has now been released from his job and conditions are much better.

The two women in charge of us are two former leaders in the Hitler Youth. They are very nice and they try to ease our lot.

21ˢᵗ June, 1947

Two years today that I vanished – what must they be thinking at home? Not a word sent out, not a word received

I made a new friend, Ellen. I don't know what brought us together, she is very intellectual and knows all the interesting people here. When the weather is fine we walk in groups round and round the parade ground. She suffers terribly, worrying about her mother. A good rumour and she is full of hope, the rumour found untrue and she is in the depth of depression. Such people are so vulnerable. Though she is ten years older than I am, I sometimes want to take her in my arms to comfort her.

Edelgard organised a white sheet for us – we don't ask where from – it costs us two rations of bread each, a big price to pay. Erni had the idea that we required blouses as a kind of family uniform. Using the simplest of styles, we can just make the sheet into four blouses. We now have to find four different colours for the embroidery – Mulle's design.

We managed to acquire small pieces of material, one in

blue, the others in red, green and yellow. By pulling out individual threads, we have the embroidery cotton. This will keep us busy and we so look forward to something pretty to wear. Needless to say, Edelgard organised the needle – a forbidden item.

July, 1947

We have a new diversion 'Reponsieren'. It is not a word at all, but it was invented by Marianne, the actress, as a joke some years ago. It now means making eye contact with the men on the other side of the fence. A few women have found their husbands here. (The woman who was arrested because of her son, has found him). If lucky, they can wave to each other from a distance, if very lucky, a word or two can be called across the fence.

Amazingly, a few boy/girl relationships have developed, both Erni and Mulle have a boyfriend, they look at each other across the wire. These boys are messengers and have the opportunity of moving from zone to zone. These jobs are a wonderful lifeline for the young boys. They get extra food, are better clothed and so have a chance to survive.

August, 1947

We have been to the theatre! It sounds quite ridiculous, but one of the buildings has a stage and a fair-sized auditorium. The Russians have allowed performances to be prepared. Marianne has recreated, from memory, a comedy she appeared in a few years ago. She has staged it and plays the leading part. Of course, the Russians love it – they attended the 'opening night'. It was a laugh, a rare thing for us.

Mid August, 1947

We have seen the first newspapers in well over two years. A copy of the "Berliner Zeitung" and "Neues Deutschland" were handed out. East German papers and one copy for two hundred women!

Our family blouses are ready – we wear them with pride!

The women who were set free from Ketschendorf – so everybody thought – were all found here. They never saw freedom. All this seeing them in the distance and waving was wishful thinking!

September, 1947

We attended a concert today! I was not sure whether I wanted to hear music under such conditions, but I went. The members of the orchestra wore black ties and dark suits – how did the Russians dress us poor prisoners in that way? Two sopranos with lovely voices sang and a solo violinist performed. I know Ilse-Veda was very upset and annoyed. She feels she should have been given the opportunity, being a soloist of some renown. The first orchestral piece, A Tschaikowsky, had quite an overwhelming effect but after that it was as if I could only take in a small offering and then it all went dull.

Late September, 1947

I went for a walk with Ellen today and we had a very disturbing conversation. She told me, in confidence, that she had a long discussion yesterday with two women who used to be employed in the Foreign Office. They claimed that the S.S. killed thousands and thousands of Jews in the various concentration camps, many in the occupied territories. Ellen said that she could not stop thinking about that revelation but had come to the conclusion that it could not be true. Preventing the Jews from holding influential posts in our country was one thing, but murder – mass murder! Neither of us can accept that Hitler could have sanctioned such evil deeds.

October, 1947

I have read a few of the newspapers that reach us from time to time. Most of it is party-political stuff which makes no sense. But there was one item which worries me. The frequent mention of food rationing in the parts of Germany occupied by the three Western Allies. Meat, butter etc., reduced by 5% or 10% - they must be starving!

An event which must mean good news, even to me! Large quantities of material were brought in and lots of volunteers sit all day cutting out and sewing trousers and coats for the men. Two sisters in our room have become the heroes, they are so good at cutting garments without patterns.

Late October, 1947

We decided to celebrate Erni's birthday on 1st November. We are saving bread and tiny quantities of sugar, butter and jam. It is all going to be a surprise for Erni. We are even making a few presents. I have a small piece of white material which I will embroider as a handkerchief.

2nd November, 1947

We really did celebrate. We started the night before with a 'bed Hupferl', a sort of night cap, a few small pieces of toast, all lovingly decorated. Breakfast was late because we wanted to take it at our leisure. We were eating off white china plates! A few of these exist, treasured by their owners, and one has to have good contacts to borrow them. We feasted on a variety of patés on bread. What wonderful illusions hunger can conjure up! Meatballs were served for lunch – more bread than meat – and a pudding to follow. Bread soaked in what here goes as coffee, mixed with a little jam and butter, well beaten, is a delicacy. The high-light of the day was the gateau – artistically decorated by Mulle – which was presented at coffee time.

We know that saving up so much food, all for just one day, is not healthy, but … …

Mid November, 1947

Small miracles happen! The Russian authorities have given us permission to organise lectures and courses. Everybody with expertise in a specialised subject has been asked to run a course. We can chose from literature, gardening, cooking, etiquette and Russian, to name a few. Only the capitalist languages, English and French, are prohibited.

As I will have to live in the Russian occupied Germany, I think it will be sensible to learn their language. Everybody seems to think the same.

End November, 1947

I am worried about Erni. She is normally full of ideas but now she says she will do one thing and then she sits on her 'bed' and stares into the distance. She will not say and we don't know, whether she is day-dreaming or whether her mind is wandering and she can no longer control it.

Our classes are not going well. We meet in groups at various corners of our room, but we have – and are not allowed to have - no papers or pens nor books or any aids. We learn words by repeating them aloud, but after a few seconds I have forgotten again. Our brains will not do the job after years of starvation.

December, 1947

There is a general rule here that after we have consumed our midday water soup, we all lie down for a rest. The lights are turned off and the room is in semi-darkness. It never gets light anyway, because the few windows are so small.

I hate sleeping during the day, I feel so miserable on awakening. So I sit up and look out into this cold, empty space. All around the walls are the bunks on which, body by body, two hundred women try to sleep to forget their sorrow, fear and hunger. Utter despair creeps over me during that hour.

23rd December, 1947

There is activity everywhere. For the first time Christmas will be celebrated by us. We have all been saving up and cake-making is all important today. We are out-doing each other in beautiful decorations. Even the Russian guards seek excuses to walk through our room to have a secretive look at our creations. They pretend not so see, as they should report us.

24th December, 1947

It is evening and all over Germany the church bells will be ringing – not a sound reaches our ears.

But then someone started "Silent Night, Holy Night" and for twenty minutes or so the sound of our treasured Christmas hymns carried across the camp – no guard came to stop this prohibited activity.

January, 1948

A Russian Commission has been inspecting our camp. Some people recognised the Doctor who is referred to as Father Christmas because of his white beard. Something usually happens after his visit – and it did. Mattresses, rather small ones, have appeared and for the first time in two and a half years we are not sleeping on blank boards. We have also received a few white sheets – what luxury!

I passed out the other day when we were standing outside for the daily counting and I am now allowed to remain on our bunk – a Russian soldierswalks through the room to count us.

Later in January, 1948

Medical examinations are in progress. It was more an inspection – the doctor looked at us in our birthday suits and those most closely resembling skeletons were announced dystrophikers, the worse cases are to receive extra food rations.

21ˢᵗ *January, 1948*

Another birthday, the third as a prisoner – I am twenty-five now! We saved our rations to celebrate with cake and an elaborate breakfast but the loveliest surprise, organised by Erni, came last night when the lights were out and we settled down to sleep. The door next to us opened and Mozart's lullaby floated through the silence – it was sung by a lovely voice – just for me!

February, 1948

Erni has at last been seen by a doctor. She never complained much to us about back pain, but they are now talking about tuberculosis of the spine. I never knew there are so many forms of TB. There is no treatment for her except that she has to move into the sick quarters, one of the small buildings in the Old Camp. She has a proper bed there, white bedding and extra food, but she has to lie quite flat and still, without even raising her head – what a shock!

Tuberculosis is so wide-spread here, no cure is available, it kills and kills!

Still February, 1948

Our family is not the same without Erni. Edelgard goes her own way much of the time, we never quite know what she is up to.

We cannot visit Erni, unless we slip in unnoticed for a moment.

March, 1948

I suffer from worms. It is awful. The first-aid assistant for our building gives me enemas which are equally awful.

It is still so cold, we have not felt warm for some months. The only way to experience some warmth is to sit on top of the pipes but then the others complain that the room is being deprived of that bit of warmth.

Early April, 1948

Ever since the Commission visited us early this year, the rumours have grown in numbers, all pointing in one way or another to our freedom. Today, we were called out for an unexpected assembly. The Russians and the interpreters brought a long list of names and those on the list had to pack their belongings and be ready to move.

Mid-April, 1948

We have suffered ten days of turmoil. Almost everybody is on the move. More lists of names are being read every day. One of the large buildings has been cleared and all those on the lists are housed there now. Those that were turned out are now taking up the vacant places elsewhere.

We are developing into two camps. The 'called' and the 'uncalled' and now a high fence has been erected, cutting us off from our friends.

End April, 1948

They say there are no more lists now! Nobody has officially said what this division means but everybody assumes that those called up will be going home. But what of us?

Mulle, Edelgard, Muttchen, Ellen, they are all on the other side of the fence!

Erni is still on this side but she is bed-ridden and cannot walk.

I had to move to one of the buildings in the Old Camp. As is happened, the first night I found myself on my own with lots of empty spaces around me on the upper gallery of the bunks. I have never been troubled much by fleas and bed bugs but that night they had no choice; it was me or nothing! I hardly slept, the bed bugs came from all sides, they dropped from the ceiling – the more I killed, the more arrived! An awful night.

May, 1948

There is one benefit – the women who feel they are about to go home have passed their unnecessary belongings to us. I have acquired a blanket, it is brown and very loosely woven. I had a good look at it and I think I can undo the weaving by pulling out the threads. Knitting needles – a forbidden item – have existed in the camp for some time. They are bicycle spokes that have been smuggled in by the new men and then been sold for bread. I have a pair in my possession; I will knit a slightly flared skirt and a jacket.

Later in May, 1948

I can speak to Erni occasionally through a window and I have had contact again with Ilse-Veda. Why is she still here? She is an older person, rather frail and has committed no crime.

I have no friends around me, but I work furiously on my knitting. Undoing the blanket is a much more time-consuming task than anticipated.

June, 1948

The sick in Erni's room have been told that they must get up and walk. The Russians will not release anybody unable to leave on their own two feet – they will just stay behind.

Erni cannot even stand on her feet after three months being confined to her bed. What an ordeal it must have been for her!

Early July, 1948

Life goes on as before, except that the high fence is separating us from our friends. Erni manages to go for short walks now and I often walk with her in the sunshine.

Mid July 1948

They say the first group of people have left the camp,

they are free! If it is true, someone at home will hear from me, both Mulle and Muttchen have memorised my address.

Late July, 1948

Yes, there are all going. The camp on the other side of the fence is almost empty. What of us? But then we have never been told why we are here, or for how long. At least I know I was a supporter, believed in Hitler, but so many have done nothing wrong except that they are Germans.

August, 1948

We saw a few more newspapers, a lot is written about Berlin and English and American aircraft flying into Berlin.

My two-piece is finished! I have something decent to wear. I inherited a pair of army boots – what luck – a pair of shoes on my feet!

21st August, 1948

After weeks of uncertainty, we had to face the bitter truth. We are on the move again. This morning we had to take our belongings – still no more than my old bag holds. Again waiting and counting and then the march. We walked this way seventeen months ago – it seems much longer – and in the distance the same long goods train! Where will it take us?

The good thing was that the sick had transport provided for them – I didn't see Erni but she did not have to walk.

It was evening before the train moved off, we sat in the dark, the train stopped, doors were opened and slammed shut again. Once again loaves of bread, chunks of margarine were pushed into the wagon and there were sausages, too. Again the worry about the sharing out, in equal portions, of the food. Hungry people can be suspicious people! But soon there was more banging of doors and much shouting – the sausages had to be returned. They were found not to be fit for consumption. Very humane to save us from food poisoning!

One Day Later

The train moved and shunted and stopped. At one time we made a short stop at a railway station and someone caught sigh of "Weimar". Not far from Weimar stands Buchenwald, one of the concentration camps I had heard of during Hitler's time. What irony, if that was our destination now!

(iv) Buchenwald

23rd September, 1948

It was hours before the doors opened and we saw daylight again. Inevitably, we waited and waited, the train was too long for the Buchenwald platform. Darkness was falling when our sad column passed through the very elaborate gate of yet another camp.

The first sight was of rows of two-storey brick houses. No longer the draughty, wooden huts of Jamlitz and Mühlberg. But then, every building is fenced off from the next one, hardly leaving any space between them. None of the wide, open areas of Mühlberg which, at least during the summer months, meant so much to us.

Every house has four rooms and in every room about fifty women are accommodated.

One great happiness. I have been re-united with Erni. We sleep in individual bunk beds with straw sacks to lie on. We secured the lower bunks and Erni is right next to me.

Next Day

Disappointment. The food is as bad as it has been for years. Water soup, bread, a tiny spoonful of butter or jam. And we still have our roll-calls every day and wait and are counted.

October, 1948

Just prior to leaving Mühlberg Erni and I acquired a large, white piece of material, a very heavy cover for a feather bed. We had a look at it now and decided to undo the weaving which should give us lots of knitting material. We consulted and the plan is to produce underwear, which we need most of all, a vest and pants combination. Then a blouse each. Erni is responsible for the design and I for the knitting.

November, 1948

Erni has been transferred to the sick room – or house- it is hardly a hospital. She tried to walk again only because of the chance of going home. Now that we are still here, her only hope is for rest and better food. I shall not be able to see her at all as she is in another building and we are all separated by those wretched fences.

We hardly ever leave the house, there is no space for walking. The only exercise we have is the weekly visit to the bath house. It is an unusual place, the water appears from many holes in the ceiling. We are always being rushed in and out, as we have no towels we dry off as we dress and if we wash our hair, we walk back whilst it is still wet.

Late November, 1948

I have nobody now as a friend. Two women in our room show rather odd behaviour. They are friends in adjacent beds and every now and then they drape blankets all around their beds and disappear behind them.

I am working non-stop on unravelling our material. I can only do an inch at a time, it is much more difficult than I expected. It is hard work and slow. Erni left me the design pattern. The blouses will have wide, long sleeves and will be gathered just below the shoulders. For the underwear we developed a fancy pattern. When shall I ever finish all that?

December, 1948

This is obviously not a very friendly camp - if concentration camps can ever be friendly. We are not allowed to hold lectures or courses. The woman in charge of us is one of these unfortunate Russian/German people, we are sure she is spying for the Russians, she looks well fed!

And now we had a big search. It was suddenly "All out". We stood in the open until a few guards came and entered the house. After they had finished our room was in a terrible mess. Even some of the straw sacks had been slit open. My knitting needles survived!

24th December, 1948

Christmas once more – the fourth! All the preparations went as in previous years, we saved and baked. We have a stove in the room and a fire is going some of the time, quite good for cooking if one manages to get near it. I am not very interested – best to treat the day like any other.

January, 1949

I speak to Ilse-Veda from time to time. She lives in the room adjacent to ours. Otherwise I keep to myself and knit.

21st January, 1949

I am twenty-six today. I just cannot help remembering the date.

February, 1949

A working party goes out every day to gather in potatoes. They were put down in beds in a field last autumn, covered with straw and soil. Now they have to be dug out.

It was my turn yesterday. It is understood that whoever goes out brings back potatoes for the others. We go prepared with sleeves tied up around the wrists and some material wrapped around our waist so that potatoes can be hidden. Of course, this is prohibited and the in-charge stands at the gate when we return and searches us. Most of the goods are lost that way and we risk punishment. I got away with it. It is really silly of us to hope that we are not detected, we are far too thin to hide anything on our bodies.

But this excursion had a most unexpected outcome for me. To handle food – even raw food – all day was too much of a temptation. Despite dirty hands and all that, I wiped the soil of some of the potatoes and ate them! We came across some onions and I bit into one like an apple. The night and this morning were dreadful. I have suffered hunger for four years now but this was almost unbearable! I can only assume that the juices of the raw vegetable made the digestive system go into overdrive. What terrible pains of hunger!

March, 1949

The camp has acquired an X-ray screen and we are all to be examined.

Later in March, 1949

It was our turn for being X-rayed. One stands in front of a fairly large screen and, to my surprise, a dark patch was found on my left lung. The Russian doctor who was present seemed quite excited about it (perhaps he has never used an X-ray screen). I am now declared a TB sufferer and must return for weekly check-ups.

Come to think of it, those men I nursed in Ketschendorf were all dying of consumption, I didn't know then.

I am now ordered to rest. I am off the cleaning rota in our room and I shall receive additional TB food rations.

I feel uneasy about my special status. There are so many TB sufferers in the camp but their complaints don't show on the screen and they are offered no help.

April, 1949

I have developed a very good way of lying on my back, my bundle of belongings behind my head, my elbows planted on the straw sack and thus carry on with my knitting. Progress on this is slow, I manage only a couple of centimetres or so per day.

May, 1949

I have only monthly check-ups now, the disease is not spreading according to the picture on the screen. Knowing a bit more now, I obviously suffered from TB in Ketschendorf when despite the cold I perspired so badly every night – how did I get over it?

June, 1949

Ilse-Veda has offered to give me English lessons. I am to visit her in her room every morning and talk to her in English. Of course, this is not allowed, no lectures or courses are allowed, certainly not in English. But, if nobody in the room gives us away, we should be all right.

Early July, 1949

We are all 'up in arms' about this woman who is in charge of us. We want to get rid of her. It was suggested we go on hunger strike by refusing to allow the food to be brought into our complex. Many object to this action, which is not surprising.

A Few Days Later

Our hunger strike has really stirred things up. Apparently, hunger strikes and suicides upset the Russians very much. Ironical really, when by their own actions they have killed thousands here! Our spokeswoman is now a Frau Gobin, she is much respected and she does know how to deal with the Russians. She shows courage and the Russians respect her for it.

Late July, 1949

Frau Gobin is now in charge. The other woman has disappeared. We think she was sent back to Russia and that constitutes punishment. The Russians use spies and traitors but they despise them. A good lesson to remember!

Skin tests for TB were taken on everybody. Mine was positive, Erni's negative – strange!

August, 1949

I am now working on our blouses, they will be very attractive.

My English lessons are going quite well. I have to make up little stories to keep the conversation going. I sit at the side of Ilse-Veda's bed and I have learnt a bit more about her. She was a child prodigy and when her musical gift was discovered her mother took her to Europe where she studied in St. Petersburg under the famous Prof. Auer and also in London. Unfortunately, she was in Germany when war broke out in 1914 and she and her mother were interned. I don't think they suffered any deprivation but they could not leave the country which hindered her career.

September, 1949

Erni has let me know that she is coming back to our room. Her bed has been kept for her all this time. Why don't I feel pleased – happy to have a friend near me again? I don't, the more I think about it, the more I dread her return. I keep puzzling about my feelings – perhaps I have withdrawn into myself much more than I ever realised. When we were four in our family it was easy to live with the others, now I want to be left to myself. Erni is such an unselfish person, I feel she will always do and suggest what she thinks are my wishes and that puts me under an obligation to do likewise. It makes life so complicated – I must not show my feelings.

October, 1949

Our food is getting better. The soup is less watery and a lump of yeast – once or twice a week – has been added to our diet. I suppose, just as yeast makes the bread rise, it will do similarly to us, i.e. blow us up! But this has opened up new ideas for our cooking: crumble the bread, add sugar and yeast and a little warm liquid, keep in a warmish place for an hour or two and you can sit down to a full bowl of bread pudding – a feast!

This new plenty is raising our spirits. The belief that we shall be home for Christmas is gaining ground.

1ˢᵗ November, 1949

Erni's birthday. We celebrated with cake and pudding – and perhaps the thought that it will be the last of such birthdays! Can one still entertain such thoughts?

I excused myself from my English lesson for today, but Ilse-Veda was very angry. She would not accept the birthday as good enough an excuse. She does not like Erni – she wants my undivided attention.

November, 1949

Our knitting has now become a frantic obsession. If and when we go home we have to have everything completed including two scarves which we have now added to our programme.

24ᵗʰ December, 1949

Everybody has been saving again and preparing the Christmas fare – our beds are turned into kitchens. But now that Christmas Eve is with us, we are strictly forbidden to sing – and we hoped to be home!

25ᵗʰ December, 1949

An extraordinary day! Word went around that a church service would be held, a Bishop would visit the camp to conduct the Christmas service. Anybody wishing to go could do so. As it turned out, only those with reasonable clothes and shoes were allowed to attend. I didn't volunteer, perhaps I should have. The hall was decorated with a Christmas tree and candles and the Bishop was the first person from the outside world we had seen for a very long time. Some witnesses said the Bishop had tears in his eyes. But typically, whilst the visitor was in the camp, we were under house arrest, not a soul visible, we did not exist!

31ˢᵗ December, 1949

So high are our spirits that some in our room suggested

celebrating the end of 1949 with a fancy-dress party! I couldn't join in, I withdrew to the far end of the room and saw a vision that left me strangely moved. I could see the men in the house opposite, they looked so grey and dejected in the dim light of a single electric bulb. Superimposed on this picture of misery was the reflection in the window of the party that was going on behind me. Two worlds – hope and despair – was it the old years and the promise of the new one?

16th January, 1950

Is it happening? Could it be?

Two Russians, with an interpreter, arrived this morning with a list of names. Those called up had to take their belongings and go. They disappeared down the road. What will tomorrow bring?

GOING HOME

17th January, 1950

We are in an isolation barrack. The Russian officers returned this morning with their list – my name was called and soon afterwards Erni's.

We had already agreed between us that we would wear all our 'precious' clothes. The new underwear, the embroidered blouse, the knitted one and the scarf (which I had only just finished) and I would also wear my woollen skirt and jacket. We expect the Russians will search us and confiscate whatever they fancy themselves.

What will tomorrow bring?

Berlin, 18th January, 1950

We are free! We are free! Never will the 18th January be forgotten.

We were woken up early, handed some provisions – and waited! One person after another was led into a an adjacent room. When it was my turn I noticed a large heap of clothing and other treasures in the middle of the room. My good, old, little bag – which had seen me through more than four years – was thoroughly inspected. The Russian woman looked at me sternly, but took nothing.

From there onto another room and more waiting. Behind a desk sat a Russian who passed me a piece of paper on which it said: '............ has been released from the internment camp and is on her way to Mahlow.'

On the reverse side someone had added: 'Money received; has no further demands.'

Then I was told to sign and the money was handed over – money I had never seen before. For four and a half years I had not handled any money. I assumed that what I was given would pay my fare home.

Out through another door. "Am I free now?" There were

lots of people milling around, newspaper reporters among them. They tried to stop us and ask questions, but we brushed past them in silence but I heard a voice saying, "Yes, we were well treated." Sad, if people read that in their papers tomorrow.

One last door and I was out in the open. I crossed a large square. "Was that reality? Me, all on my own and free?"

At the far end of the square a bus was waiting, it was not long and Erni joined me. The bus set off in the direction of Weimar. When Goethe lived here Weimar was a famous cultural centre, now it will forever be linked to Buchenwald whose walls saw the suffering imposed on human beings by Hitler and then by Stalin.

It was already dark when we reached the railway station. Could we just go to the ticket office and ask for a ticket? Well, only we saw something unusual in doing that. And, yes, there was a train due for Berlin at 5.00 p.m.

We were four of us leaving for Berlin. We found seats in an ill-lit compartment where the blinds were let down. Before I had time to think what I was saying I heard my voice "This is just as it was in the war!"

All our fellow travellers looked up and gazed at us. To them it was, of course, an odd remark to make. I believe they guessed where we came from. They asked no questions but were very kind to us.

We reached Berlin and there was the Red Cross looking out for us. Last night's arrivals had prepared them. The ladies were so concerned, they took us to a hostel in Dahlem, we slept in a soft bed between white sheets and a cup of cocoa was brought to our bedside.

19th January, 1950

19th January, 1950

We woke up to our first day of freedom! After breakfast we left this sanctuary and suddenly realised that we had to face life, real life! Going home was our aim, but what if the loved ones where no longer there? Our first day may, after all, prove a very painful one.

We walked into the nearest Police station and asked whether we could be told if certain families lived at a given address. No, they could not, it was not their duty. But when we explained that we had just come from Buchenwald it all changed, they could not do enough for us. Yes, Erni's mother was registered at the old address, but there was nothing they could tell me. I realised what it meant living in West or East Berlin and worse to have one's home outside Berlin in the DDR. Before we left the officers had a whip-round and we set off with enough West marks to pay our bus fares.

We also learnt that near the Potsdamer Platz there is a Refugee Centre for those fleeing the East. I think we made a mistake, we thought registering at the Centre might help us in the weeks to come. But there were hundreds of people, all refugees from the DDR and we waited in a queue for hours. The treatment was so impersonal that we felt totally deflated and, worse, when we finally emerged from the Centre it was already dark and I didn't dare risk taking Erni home, as I had wanted to do. So we parted and I set off alone to find my home. Waiting for the train I was suddenly full of fear. I did not want to be recognised by anybody. Did not want to be drawn into a conversation. This last part of my home-coming I had to do in solitude. I had to find for myself whether home was still what I hoped it would be.

I saw one person looking at me intently, so I sneaked away and reached Mahlow. Nothing seemed changed, through the barrier, down the stairs, turn right and then along the dark, unmade road until our house came in sight. Lights shone across!

I stopped outside the house and bent down to inspect the name plate. Yes, our name was still there.

I put my bag down by the gate, rang the bell and stepped inside, into the dark.

After a few moments the door opened and there stood my uncle! He looked around, walked to the gate and as he saw my bag I was in his arms.

I was home. I was safe!

And then it was all such a whirl. There were my aunt and my cousin with a baby in her arms and her husband and a little boy.

I was told my brother had returned from the war only last year, that he would be home from work any minute, that he was engaged and that his fiancée was living in our house.

Soon my brother arrived, my aunt went out to prepare him and then we were in each other's arms.

FREE AGAIN – ALMOST

20ᵗʰ January, 1950

After four and a half years there is much to catch up with.

Our house is rather over-populated. My aunt and uncle use the large bedroom and the dining room. Traute and her family have Mum's bedroom and my little room. Jurgen sleeps in the lounge and his fiancée, Helga, in his bedroom.

My arrival must have necessitated a hurried family conference. Helga has moved into the lounge and I have my brother's little room.

The little boy I met last night is a foster child that my aunt and uncle are looking after. He was a baby who was separated from his parents when they were fleeing from the Russians. The Red Cross cannot find the parents.

It appears my uncle returned home soon after my arrest and when they were evicted from their flat they moved into our house. The oracle in Ketschendorf was correct! How strange! I admire my uncle, he used to be a bank clerk and was not very practical. Now he works for the local Council as an Inspector. In all weathers he has to get on his bicycle and visit the neighbouring villages and check that the farmers fulfil their norm, i.e. hand over to the State whatever they have been ordered to produce. The farmers are not pleased with that arrangement but it seems that my uncle manages to get on with them and his employers.

Eileen and her children moved out when my relatives moved in. Her husband returned from the concentration camp in 1948.

My aunt Anne was taken back to her flat in Berlin and died later of cancer.

My uncle Paul is also dead, he was found at the end of the war with a pistol in his hand.

Jurgen was taken prisoner in Russia, handed over to the Poles and only returned home last year. But he was able to write and learned of Mum's death and my fate before he arrived back. I cannot ask him how he felt when he read that news. He is now employed in a Ministry in Berlin. Aunt Lisa helped him to find that job. He was 25 when he returned home and had nothing but his school certificates. He could not face depending for years on his relatives in order to train for a profession.

Muttchen and Mulle kept their word. They wrote and my family knew that I was still alive, at least in 1948.

21st January, 1950

My birthday. The first since 1943, which I am spending at home. Everybody had a present for me. Aunt Lisa arrived in the afternoon. What a reunion! She had promised Mum to look after us – why did Mum think she might not survive the war? I sometimes think of our landlady in Ruhpolding. She would not say what she saw in Mum's handlines. Did she see her early death?

24th January, 1950

Today I have to call on our Council Offices to claim my food rationing coupons. Everything, except bread, is still in very short supply and rationed. I went with great misgivings, I assumed that all the people working there would be good communists and how would they treat me?

As I entered the office I faced a woman - I did not recognise her - but an expression of pleasure passed over her face and she called out, "Ah, our Inge is back!" It really moved me!!

On the way back I had planned to visit my aunt Edith, she has remarried. I rang the bell but a stranger answered and did not seem very pleased with my request. No, my aunt had moved a few years ago!

31st January, 1950

I had to visit a lady doctor today. My body has not been

functioning in some departments. Fortunately she believes in nature cures and will order massage and hot baths!

7th February, 1950

My uncle is trying to find me a job. I have an interview with a local firm, KWU Handelsgesellschaft.

9th February, 1950

Hurrah, I have a job! What luck!

Though the office consists of a number of wooden huts, it is surrounded by trees – quite idyllic. I shall have a thirty minute walk, almost over fields. We start at 7 o'clock in the morning.

10th February, 1950

I was in Berlin to visit Erni and met her mother and brother. Her father died soon after the war. What a shock for Erni, she was very close to her father – he died five years ago – and she did not know!

How different West Berlin is. The shops are full of food and everything one could wish for. There is nothing in our shops.

I was told that from the moment the new currency was introduced in the West – one for East Germany and one for the West – the shops were full. In our DDR the basic food stuffs are very inexpensive. Fares are almost pre-war prices, but there is nothing else. No clothes, coffee, chocolate, just nothing. One could buy in the West, but a) we are not allowed to and b) when exchanging money, we have to give ten of our marks for one mark of West money. In other words, my monthly salary would buy 20 bars of chocolate and nothing else.

Now I understand why the DDR newspapers which we read in 1948 reported that food rations in the West were reduced by such and such a percentage. There was so much food about in the shops that rationing became meaningless. How statistics can lie!

15th February, 1950

My first day at work. It went very well but what a strange firm it is. One department sells china etc., goods produced in little factories in Thuringia. Another sells alcohol (mostly liqueur) to the local trade and my department is called the Textile Department. In reality we are the depository for all the goods confiscated from people who had been shopping in the West. At our railway station there is always a police control and everybody who arrives by train has to show the identity papers and the contents of bags and cases. Goods bought in the West are taken away. I feel a cold shiver going down my spine whenever I see the Russians standing there! We have to register all the goods that come into our department and eventually the local authority will release them to local traders for sale.

My boss is quite nice - the Head of the firm is a very imposing man, good-looking and very authoritarian!

End February, 1950

Jurgen told me that when he had returned home he went to the authorities and demanded to know what had happened to me. Of course, he did not receive a reply but instead he was warned that he should keep his mouth shut or he would find himself without a job.

March, 1950

Erni suggested that we attend a meeting in West Berlin for all former inmates of the concentration camps. She thought it was our duty to go and that it would be nice to meet old fellow sufferers – the idea seems good.

We gathered in a very large hall which was crowded, but the whole thing was a fiasco. Two organisations have been formed and both claim to represent the interests of the victims of the Russian concentration camps. They are now great rivals and the two leaders fought a verbal war which was very unpleasant for us. We should not have attended!

End March, 1950

I went to the Potsdamer Platz today. A part of Berlin which I knew so well. It is a foreign world now, most of the familiar buildings have disappeared, others are ruins. The Reichskanzlei has completely gone. Then there is the Tiergarden, once such a popular park – there are no trees left – the Berliners cut them down for firewood – it is all so sad.

But the Potsdamer Platz is famous now because here East and West meet. On the West side the stalls sell all the goods one longs to buy, but we cannot as we have no money. The frontier line is not marked but one cannot fail to see where it is. We live on the poverty side!

Good Friday, late in the evening

Last Saturday I queued up at the Staat Opera to purchase tickets for 'Parsival' for myself and my aunt. She loves opera but her family is not interested.

We had good seats in the stalls but as soon as the curtain rose I felt some dreadful stomach ache and knew I would faint. I got up but had to push past a long row of people with whom I was not very popular. I made the door and remember the handle slipping from my fingers and vaguely heard the crash of the door closing behind me. Then I was out. I spent the whole evening in the First Aid room. I was all right by the time the opera finished. What a disappointment! Perhaps the excitement of it was too much for me. My poor aunt!

April, 1950

Next week I must visit my uncle Walter in West Berlin. I have not seen him for years and don't know his second wife. I hope it will not be embarrassing. There was a bit of a family quarrel. But he is my Godfather. In the years gone by he used to have me in tears. He was never a Nazi and the things he used to say hurt my feelings but I lacked the gift of arguing against him. Maybe I should have listened to him a bit more.

Middle of April, 1950

My visit was quite a success. We left the past behind us and sat and talked. Much discussed in the West is the film 'The Third Man'. I also heard for the first time about the Berliner Air Lift which came to an end only last year. Now I understand why the DDR papers ignored it. West Berlin is such a small island within the DDR and there are only two or three roads which connect it and on those are check points, controlling entry and exit. In June 1948 the Russians closed those points obviously intending to starve the population of Berlin so that the Russians could annex that part of Berlin. But the Western powers would not allow this to happen, the British and Americans flew in, by day and by night, everything that the town required to survive. After a year Stalin had to admit defeat and open the roads again. How the political situation has changed in five years!

My uncle lives with his in-laws because he is unemployed. Unemployment and lack of accommodation are a great problem in the West. That made me think. In January, when I registered as a refugee, I was told that within six months I could, at any time, abscond to the West. I never considered doing so, our house and my brother are in Mahlow, but if I did so, where would I go, where to find work, who could help me?

It was an interesting evening. I arrived home by the last train at 1.00 a.m. The walk home is along a dark, unmade road, but that did not worry me but I did dread the Russian guards at the station, even though I had no forbidden goods on me.

22nd April, 1950

Aunt Edith's birthday. We were quite a gathering for afternoon coffee. When we were all sitting around the table I started talking about the camp years, everybody listened in silence. I never spoke of my experiences before, it just poured out of me. It was so selfish especially as one of the ladies present had a husband who had not returned from the camps. It seems there are occasions when one does not know what one is doing until it is too late.

May, 1950
I have found Ilse-Veda. She lives in one furnished room in a nice part of West Berlin. She is not very happy and has already fallen out with her landlady.

June, 1950
Jurgen is getting married. A baby is on the way. My aunt and uncle are looking for a flat of their own.

There are far too many of us in the house; I noticed that last night when I was left to cook my uncle's supper. We have two small electric rings for three families. Mum had opted for cooking with gas and since the end of the war there has been no gas available here – because it comes from the West!

July, 1950
Once every month all offices remain closed here and we all gather at the Council Offices for a political lecture. It is very boring as all the communist speakers can do no more than thrash out political slogans. But this week our Head of the firm was invited to lecture on economics and business management. It was wonderful! He made it quite clear what he thought of the communist principles but did it so cleverly that nobody could accuse him of running down the system! He is a very remarkable man!

August, 1950
In the office, tickets were offered for an open-air concert by Russian dancers and singers. I bought a ticket but soon found that nobody else had done so. They all thought that we should boycott these Russian attempts at being friendly and were very surprised that I, of all people,

should support their efforts. I had not thought of it that way, I do not hate the Russians, only the Bolshevik system. Now I am rather confused and ashamed.

Later in August 1950

I went again to Ilse-Veda. She has heard from her husband. He survived five years in the concentration camp but has not been freed. It is now known that about 3000 people were held back by the Russians and are now to face a German court. He has been condemned to another 25 years in jail all because he held a position in Dr. Goebbels' Propaganda Ministry. But he is allowed to receive one parcel a month, but Ilse-Veda has hardly enough money to feed herself.

I also learnt that Frau Bechler was condemned to death – and her husband is a Minister in our government – unbelievable!

September, 1950

Jurgen informed me a little while ago that we inherited a few shares from my mother. As we are the poor DDR dwellers the bank in the West is allowing us to sell our shares (of course devalued to one tenth of the former value). Jurgen has sold and we now possess a few west marks!

We have agreed that our first duty will be to have our mother's name added to our father's gravestone. Then there will, hopefully, be enough money left for me to buy a pair of shoes and a piece of material for a badly needed dress.

Early October, 1950

Aunt and uncle have moved into a nice flat. Jurgen occupies the large bedroom and the lounge. I have moved into the dining room and sleep on the settee. Heating will be a problem. We have not enough fuel and my sister-in-law is not capable of dealing with the fireplace in the hall which was designed to heat both the downstairs rooms. I shall be sitting in a cold room!

24th October, 1950

My sister-in-law is in hospital and gave birth to a boy. Jurgen is very proud. I will look after my brother for the coming week but I do not intend to become the unpaid nurse-maid. I am beginning to enjoy my freedom. I can do and go where I like and I want it to stay that way. I have never before been so free from obligations and it is only the political system and my lack of money that impose any restrictions.

November, 1950

I went with Erni to the State Opera to hear Helge Roswaenge in 'Il Trovatore'. He was always one of my heart-throbs. A few weeks ago we heard him in 'The Land of Smiles'. It was sad to see such a famous singer in an operetta. So it was important to us to hear him in an opera. The applause was tremendous as soon as he stepped onto the stage and he was transformed into the old Roswaenge, he had to repeat the great aria from the last act – it was wonderful.

25th December, 1950

I spent Christmas Eve with my aunt and uncle. I don't know whether Jurgen expected me to be with them but it was his first Christmas with a family and I thought they should be left alone.

Went to Erni today.

18th January, 1951

Our Freedom Day!

Erni and I will always celebrate this day. It is good to remember. We are already taking for granted so many things which a year ago were so special. In our DDR food is not plentiful and it is very dull but I no longer dream of drinking potato water.

I often think back to those camp years. We were sure

that we were suffering a great injustice being exposed to hunger and illness, robbed of our freedom and nobody seeming to care.

I remember the conversation in Mühlberg when I heard for the first time that during the Hitler years mass murder was committed and how I refused to believe that that had been possible. But now everybody knows about it and I accept it as truth. How can any human being perpetrate such cruelty, witness such evil and see thousands perish? But then I recall that we were taught that the Jews were foreigners in our country and should not be allowed to exercise any influence. How easily I was indoctrinated. How blind I was in my enthusiasm. How I tried to explain away that which appeared to be wrong and unjust.

Yes, I still think that it was a crime what Stalin did, rounding up thousands of Germans, leaving them to starve to death. Many of them had committed no wrong, had no other guilt but to be German. But now I am glad that I was amongst those who had to take the punishment and suffer and I count it an almost undeserved luck that I survived and suffered no damage to my health. But if I was guilty of supporting Hitler and his regime so I took some punishment – whether this was adequate, others will have to judge.

21st January, 1951

To celebrate my birthday I invited all my relatives for afternoon coffee. It was a stupid idea, with a ration book for one person one cannot entertain 12 people with cakes and coffee. I still apply concentration camp values and forget that people from the West are used to better things.

23rd January, 1951

I took a walk across to Blankenfelde to congratulate Val's mum on her birthday. Val is in West Germany and cannot be here. Apparently it is very difficult to obtain the Russians' permission to visit the DDR. Some people cross the border without a permit, but it is very dangerous. So I am going as daughter substitute.

At the party I met Val's aunt whose two daughters are in England, doing domestic work and they like it very much. As I was on my way out, the aunt said to me, "Why don't you go to England? It would be just right for you. Let me know if you want any advice."

On the walk home I could not stop thinking about that.

Early March, 1951

I still have a week's holiday due to me. I read about a travel agency offering a week in Thuringia. Memories of happy childhood days came flooding back. I always wished I could see the mountains in the snow.

I booked a week in Thuringia.

Thuringia, Middle March, 1951

It is all a bit different from what I expected – not surprising – this being the DDR. There was nobody at the station in Berlin to put us on the train. It was not even 'us' – just 'me'. The same at the other end, nobody there but a little boy with a toboggan for my luggage. We walked for a whole hour through the snow. I am staying with a family. There are very nice but as all people here very poor. My room is cold and the food very basic. What am I doing with myself now?

Two Days Later

I stayed in every afternoon and evening. Sitting in the living room and writing letters. Now the landlord has asked me if I wouldn't rather go out? Tomorrow I must take myself for a long walk.

Next Day

I did go for my walk – a very long one! Below the village I could see a valley and a road stretching into the distance. I had put my boots on and marched along the road until I thought it was time to turn round for my return. The sun was already setting behind the mountains when I came to a junction which I had not noticed before. I turned to the left but when the road started going uphill I knew I had been wrong. Should I turn round? It was getting dark. Then I saw a house in the distance and decided to knock and ask. Yes, I had to retrace my steps. It was dark now, only the stars illuminated my way and – I was afraid. As nobody could hear me I sang at the top of my voice to forget my fear. In the end I had to climb up a steep slope through deep snow to reach the village. I pretended that I had had a wonderful day.

The Last Day of My Holidays

Now for compensation!

When I woke the sun was rising over the mountains and the world around me was sparkling and glistening. Frost covered every blade of grass, every twig on the trees. It was the fairyland I had hoped for.

Two hours later, when I strolled along the valley and the little stream that was bubbling along, the snow had already turned to water. The grass was straightening up in the sunshine and some tiny flowers turned their heads towards the warmth. I was observing the miracle of nature.

But the thought of England was with me throughout the week.

Home Again.

I will write to Val's aunt and ask her to see whether her daughters can find me a family in England – it won't commit me to anything.

End March, 1951

Traute and her family have moved out. They found a little flat just around the corner from us. Now the Local

Authority have informed us that 4 bedrooms for three adults and a baby are too many – we have to let two rooms – this is the workers' paradise!

April, 1951

I heard from a family in England. They have a farmhouse in a small village in Oxfordshire. They would want me to look after their four children. I would be a Mother's Help and earn £2 a week. They would pay my fare and, if I stay a full year, also my return fare. But they have to apply for a work permit and that can take some months.

I decided to take the next step and say 'yes, please'. If I go it will only be for one year and then I may be able to spend a year in France and with the language knowledge I gained I would have a better chance to acquire a good job in West Germany.

20th April, 1951

This date will never be wiped from my memory: Hitler's birthday. How we adored him and now I know that he misused our trust. Whilst we believed every one of his words and followed him blindly, he ordered the murder of millions of Jews. I wonder whether he sometimes woke during the night and felt the unimaginable horrors and the pain of those people? Did he every think of those millions and millions around the world who lost possessions and life because of a war which he started?

And yet, I cannot take back or alter the enthusiasm which guided all my thoughts and deeds during those early years of my life even though I now know that my feelings were so greatly misplaced.

End April, 1951

I told Jurgen of my plans. His reaction was a bit surprising. "Oh, good. We shall be able to smoke English cigarettes." Nobody must hear of my plans. In this wonderful country one becomes a spy or traitor if one has any contact with the 'capitalists' in the West. All my letters are being posted in West Berlin – rather costly for me – and replies will go to my friends there.

I had to take a day off from work to apply for a passport in West Berlin. I shall get to know Berlin because all my visits to the authorities will be done on foot. I cannot afford bus fares.

A problem – I have to be registered as being resident in Berlin in order to be entitled to apply for a passport. i.e. I have to have a 'second address'. Now I have to find someone who owns a house and is willing to sign the official registration form confirming that I am resident there. But I don't know anybody who owns a house! My uncle is a lodger in his in-laws rented flat – would their landlord sign for me? How terribly complicated!

Early May 1951

Another day off! I now have a signature on the registration form and a stamp from the police – next for a passport!

June, 1951

A sad day in the office! A family tried to escape to West Berlin taking all their possessions with them, which were packed on a trailer. They had chosen for their route a rather remote country lane which leads directly into West Berlin. The idea was to drive up to the frontier, put the foot down on the accelerator and make a dash into freedom. Unfortunately, the car got across but not the trailer. The police brought the trailer, fully laden, to us and we had to spend the whole day unloading, unpacking, counting, indexing and storing. I feel so sad for the family.

End June, 1951

I have yet another problem – I have to give three months

notice to my employers and can only do it at the end of the quarter, i.e. if I wish to finish at the end of September I have to hand in my notice on 30th June. I shall have to risk it because otherwise I shall not be able to leave until the end of the year and that may be too late for the family in England.

July, 1951

I collected my passport – that feels very good! The next step is applying for a visa for England, more west marks needed. There are crowds of money changers at the Potsdamer Platz where one can change money. The banks don't really trade in east marks.

Middle of July, 1951

One of my colleagues – he drives our van – often visits my office. He said, "One of these days I will take you to the cinema and then we shall have real sausages and Sauerkraut at the Potsdamer Platz." (Obviously the west side). He is a married man and I should have said 'no' straight away especially as I don't care that much for him. But it is a new sensation for me to find that someone is paying me attention and it is quite a pleasant feeling.

Still July, 1951

Erni took a day off and is going to spend it with me at the Rangsdorfer Lake. During the war Jurgen and I had a little rowing boat there. Of course it has long disappeared but we hope to hire a boat for the day. The lake is big enough to idle away a day in the sunshine. We managed the rowing quite well and then allowed ourselves to drift into the reeds. Unfortunately, we were rather late in becoming aware of another boat approaching us and then, to our horror, we saw the Russian soldiers in it. There was no escaping – Erni froze with terror. No doubt we were at their mercy! Luck had it that they were decent men, our expressions probably conveyed to them our fear – they turned and rowed away. But the day was ruined and I doubt whether Erni will ever visit me again.

August, 1951

The British visa has been stamped into my passport – now for a transit visa for Holland, I shall be travelling through that country. No end to the difficulties!

Sunday, 13th August, 1951

Erni and I queued all night for theatre tickets. One has to be there when the box office opens if one wants to see something special. If was fun, we had a long, interesting conversation with a man who said he was an art critic who seems to spend his life attending plays, films, concerts and opera and then writes about them. Quite fascinating!

September, 1951

Another visa required. As I shall be flying out of Berlin (nobody travels by car, if at all possible.) I have to have a transit visa just in order to fly from Berlin to Hamburg. They say the authorities insist on this in case the aircraft has an emergency landing in the DDR. Another trip to Berlin for me and more west money!!

30th September, 1951

This is officially my last working day. All my colleagues are so very nice. I feel ashamed that I cannot dare tell them what my plans are. Only my nearest relatives know and I trust they will keep their mouths shut – for their own good as well as mine!

My boss asked me if I could stay on for another month – that is wonderful! I am still without a date for my flight – soon I will not have a penny in my pocket.

October, 1951

Ilse-Veda gave a concert in her local Town Hall. She insisted that I should attend and, of course, I did. The hall was almost full. I admire her courage and determination – she must be near to seventy and coming back after those dreadful years in the camp!

She is not pleased that I am going to England. She considers it is a country without possibilities. She would send me to America!

Mid-October, 1951

My work permit has arrived! The letter went to Erni's address and they are asking as to when I want to travel – they will then send my tickets. I have no idea how much time I will have to allow for the booking and forwarding of the papers. I have opted for the 17th November. It is a Saturday and I could spend the weekend with Ellen in Hamburg – it would be such a bonus to see her again – and I could continue by train on the Monday.

I will reply to that effect and give my uncle's address in Neu-Köln for forwarding the tickets.

End October, 1951

I now have all the visas that I shall require and even a pass which allows me to remain in West Berlin for forty-eight hours – very generous!

1st November, 1951

Now I am out of work and my last salary of 200 marks (east) will have to last me until I set off on my journey.

9th November, 1951

Jurgen is in Zechlin on a four-week training course - Political I suppose. If I am leaving on the 17th he will not be back. I have decided that I must visit him next Sunday.

Monday, 12th November, 1951

What a day I had yesterday! I met my brother even though it meant that I had to walk 5 km from the nearest railway station. We had a few hours together – something that hardly every happened since our childhood. Under his hard exterior there is a very soft heart and a caring brother. Jurgen walked with me for a good way on my return and then I continued on my own to catch the evening train. I do not possess such a luxury as a wrist-watch but the thought that I could miss the train never entered my mind – until I heard a train approaching from behind me. I was a few hundred metres from the station and reached as the train departed – it was the last one on that day!

There was nothing left for me to do but go into the station pub and ask about a room for the night. Everybody gazed at me, with some amusement. Yes, there were two small rooms available – but more money wanted! I arrived home after having to pay for my train journey as they would not accept my day-return ticket – oh dear! Oh dear!

Wednesday, 14th November, 1951

I had a strange letter from my aunt in Neu-Köln – she wants to tell me something interesting. I am visiting Erni today so I will go on Saturday.

Thursday, 15th November, 1951

I said good-bye to Erni today. Our friend, the art critic was with her. After supper he determined that he would read to us Oscar Wilde's 'Ballad of Reading Gaol'. When it came to midnight I had to interrupt him, which annoyed him very much. 'Great literature, is more important than a last train' I was informed. Yet, he entrusted me with an interesting task. In December a new opera 'Billy Budd' will be premiered in London. It is by a British composer Benjamin Britten. I am to go and hear that opera and then report back to him about the music and my impressions. The fact that I shall not live in London is of no importance to him.

Saturday, 17th November, 1951

What a stupid, foolish person I am! What a dreadful day!

It was almost 12 noon when I arrived in Neu-Köln,. My aunt opened the door with the words "Inge, there was a Registered letter for you."

I froze, terror seized me. In that second I knew it all. When my aunt wrote, sending her letter from West Berlin to the DDR she was super careful and I was incredibly stupid. That letter contained my flight tickets and today, the day I had quoted as my departure date. Worse, in true German fashion, the postman had not handed the letter to my aunt, only I, the addressee was entitled to receive it. So I rushed off to the Post Office reaching it just before closing time. In my hands I held my flight tickets, just as the aircraft was taking off from Tempelhof!

What now? I cursed the system that frightens people so much that they dare not state in a letter what they want to say for fear the letter might be opened by the authorities; the system that cuts off telephone lines so that one cannot speak from one end of the town to the other; that makes its people so distrustful of each other that they dare not confide in a neighbour lest he was a spy.

Here I am now, caught between East and West.

Then I remembered that someone had warned me that an air ticket loses its validity when the booking has not been cancelled in good time. Not even in months could I save enough money to pay for a flight to Hamburg.

With an aching heart I returned and consulted with my relatives. They advised me to go to the airport straight away. I found a BEA employee who patiently listened to my unlikely story. I must have looked so crestfallen, he took my tickets and returned after a while with them and the words, "You can fly on Monday."

I wanted to embrace him.

TO A NEW LIFE

Sunday, 18th November, 1951

I said farewell to my family, packed my case (not that there was much to pack) and now I am ready to leave, except for one last step which I dread, because if it goes wrong all my plans fail.

I have decided to leave the DDR officially instead of just getting on a train and disappearing. So today I must adhere to the regulations and go to the police and tell them that I am leaving. I was told that the police will accept that, if one can produce documents showing that the West has agreed to this relocation. I have this piece of paper which states that I can reside in West Berlin for 48 hours, but, but … … my uncle has offered to come with me, so I will at least have a witness if I should disappear again.

Now, in the stillness of the evening, it seems very strange to me that tomorrow I shall be on my way to England. In the days gone by we were never taught to hate the English, on the contrary, they were called our blood brothers, but during the war they were made into the bad Imperialists and Capitalists and now one family there will entrust their children to me!

Very strange is that now, looking back, I cannot recall a single moment when I, after serious thought, decided to take this momentous step and leave my home. I was more like a sleep-walker, like someone drawn by a magnet, and now it is too late to change my plans.

On board ship, Tuesday 20th November, 1951, 1.00 a.m.

That was a very long day!

There was much sadness in my heart when I closed the door behind me and slowly turned my back on the house which my parents so longed to leave for their children. Nobody waved a last good-bye.

My uncle was at the station, we called at the police in

Blankenfelde – all went well. It was a load off my mind. A farewell kiss from my uncle and I was on my way to the airport.

How I was looking forward to that flight! For the first time in an aircraft! All problems were forgotten. The aircraft rose between the houses, I saw Berlin below me, recognised one or two landmarks and then we were above the clouds swimming like huge feather-beds, glowing in the sun.

Ellen was at the airport, we spent an hour in a little café, I ordered the largest piece of gateau, almost dripping with cream, something I had not seen for years. I could have eaten two or three such cakes but it was obvious Ellen had lived in freedom and luxury for three years – she had forgotten!

The train journey passed without any excitements and now I am on the boat, the harbour lights faded in the distance but I am much too awake to go to bed. The night is clear and mild and I am watching the white, frothy wake of the ship disappearing into the darkness.

Then a young man joined me, we started talking. He is a member of the Concertgebouw Orchestra – how terribly exciting – they are on a tour of England. I fear I robbed the poor man of an hour of his sleep but it was such a joy for me.

Now a new day is breaking.

Tuesday, 20th November, 1951 – afternoon

I slept for a few hours, then it was by train to London. What a huge station Liverpool Street station is! And so many people! A man from Thomas Cook met me and put me into a taxi. The driver was so nice, he pointed out Buckingham Palace and drove through Hyde Park and then deposited me at Paddington Station.

There I was instructed to ask for "Reading, please." But my "Reading" sounded like "Reading a book" but one clever person understood me, corrected me, and so, with my first English lesson, my new life commenced!